Quilts
and
Quilting

Quilts and Quilting

from Threads

The Taunton Press

Cover photo by Susan Kahn

First printing: November 1991
Printed in the United States of America

A THREADS Book

THREADS magazine® is a trademark of The Taunton Press, Inc.
registered in the U.S. Patent and Trademark Office.

The Taunton Press
63 South Main Street
Box 5506
Newtown, CT 06470-5506

Library of Congress Cataloging-in-Publication Data

Quilts and quilting from Threads magazine.
      p.   cm.
   "A Threads book"—T.p. verso.
   includes index.
   ISBN 1-56158-025-2
   1. Quilting—Patterns.   I. Threads magazine
TT835.Q549   1991   91-30950
746.46—dc20   CIP

Contents

Introduction

aking quilts is a way of handing down traditions, of expressing new ideas, of stitching together the myriad threads of our lives. In this series of articles drawn from the first 35 issues of *Threads* magazine, more than two dozen master quiltmakers generously share their ideas and techniques.

We hope you'll find new inspiration and some welcome tips, whether you want to play with color and piecing, refine your hand stitches, improvise, embellish or work with geometric precision. Explore computer-generated imagery or master traditional techniques; there's a bit of it all in this rich collection. Enjoy!

— Betsy Levine, editor

This complex piece, "Walking to the Moon" (35 in. x 43 in., 1989), is a variation of the zigzag pattern. (Photo by Susan Kahn)

Big Prints, Little Pieces
A color study for quiltmakers

by Susan Sawyer

I began doing very small patchwork in 1979 while constructing fabric-covered boxes with pieced tops. I wanted the pieced parts, which were only 3 or 4 in. sq., to be interesting to look at. At first I used templates and some of the many patterns made possible with just squares and triangles. Marking around templates and cutting out each piece with scissors is a very slow process—strip piecing was in the air. Having gone to school in Florida, I'd seen a lot of Seminole Indian clothing and admired its intricacy. I got out the paper cutter.

As a printmaker, I learned that limitations can be liberating. I thought I might get to a new and interesting place if I chose a path and stayed with it, instead of trying one new thing after another. I knew that I wanted to find out about color, to work small, and to think very little about pattern for a while, so I chose the ½-in. square. Ten years later, I'm still cutting cloth into 1-in. strips to make ½-in. squares.

The box tops eventually got too confining, so in 1984 I turned to tiny quilts that get framed. There's a binding, and there's fabric on the back, but since the surface has a lot going on, quilting seems superfluous. I hand-quilt only pieces that are going in shows and any that are bigger than about 12 in. sq. I'm currently experimenting with machine quilting to cut down on time.

The combination of the elemental simplicity and endless possibility of the small squares has kept me interested. I can make the shifts and jumps of color progressions be the focus of the work. Seen in such small pieces, printed fabric changes character—each small portion of a large-scale print is different, and you get only a taste of a small-scale pattern. The colors and patterns blend into each other, as the bits of glass in a mosaic do. I've made the "Trip Around the World" pattern (photos, pp. 10 and 12; instructions, p. 11) dozens of times. It satisfies some visual need that I have for focus and symmetry.

Quiltmaking

When I start working on a quilt, I number the quilt squares on graph paper. Each number represents a fabric. Next I arrange the fabrics in a series to correspond to the numbers. Using a paper template, I cut a rough rectangle 8½ in. by 10½ in. on the straight grain of each fabric. I then press the rectangles and stack three of them together. For "Trip Around the World," I cut them into eight 1-in. by 10-in. strips with the paper cutter.

I'm limited in the length of the strips by my 12-in. paper cutter. I hope to have a bigger one someday, but for now, the 10-in. strips are easy to handle and can be stored on cardboard-box bottoms in a big drawer. The cutter blade has to be extremely sharp. Fine pima cottons can't be cut at all with a dull blade, but domestic cottons are more forgiving. Most people who do strip piecing use a rotary cutter and a mat. I do, too, when I'm making something out of normal-sized pieces, but a rotary cutter isn't as ac-

To cut her 1-in.-wide fabric strips quickly and accurately, Susan Sawyer uses a sharp paper cutter (left). Above, she pins strips together for sewing, keeping the piles of neatly arranged strips at hand. (Photos by Mary Galpin Barnes)

By using large-scale prints in small pieces, Sawyer achieves a kaleidoscopic effect that disguises the traditional pattern. "Trip Around the World," 1989, 7 in. x 7 in. (Photo by Len Mastri)

curate or as fast as a paper cutter for the kind of work that I'm doing.

I hold down the cloth and keep it from shifting under the blade with a strip of basswood, ¾ in. wide by 12 in. long by ³⁄₁₆ in. thick, and unplaned on the back, which is fuzzy enough to hold the cloth. A piece of Masonite with felt glued on the back works too. A hymnal alongside the cutter holds up the cloth being cut off—it's just the right height and size.

After I cut the strips, I lay them out into the groups that will be stitched together. Arranging the groups for "Trip Around the World" is easy enough that I can do it without numbering the fabric strips.

Sewing the strips together couldn't be simpler; I'm just careful to keep the seams absolutely straight. Several layers of electrician's tape on the bed of the machine just less than ¼ in. from the needle serve as a guide, and I stitch rather slowly, which isn't hard on my Singer treadle machine. It's modern for a treadle—with a detachable motor and light—but I prefer foot power. The leg motion makes it bearable to sit at the machine for hours. I've learned that the thread tension has to be perfectly ad-

justed to prevent the seams from curving and puckering, that the feed dog and bobbin areas have to be clean, and that the #11 needle has to be sharp. Either of the last two problems can make the seams just a hair bigger, and in a piece that's 60 squares wide, that's a disaster!

As I finish each seam, I finger-press the seam allowances away from the needle. I sew up to 10 or 12 strips together, depending on what the pattern requires; more than that is hard to handle.

I press open all seams to eliminate bulk and increase accuracy. These quilts don't go on beds and aren't subject to stress, so I don't have to worry about them coming apart. I then cut the now-striped pieces of sewn cloth crosswise into 1-in.-wide strips with the paper cutter, discarding the ends, which are never good enough to use.

Before sewing together these strips, I pin in the next-to-the-end squares, and in the middle of the strip, too, if the strips are long. After stitching, I press open the seams again. It's mainly because of all this ironing that I try to avoid synthetics and blends. They're likely to shrink if I forget where they are and press them on the cotton setting.

After sewing on one or more borders, I cut a piece of backing fabric, pin the top and backing layers together, and machine-sew on the binding, which is made of four 1¼-in.-wide strips. I make simple Amish-style square corners and handsew the binding to the back.

Lately I've been doing some much larger pieces, in variations of the zigzag (photo, p. 8). These can get complicated, so I make a drawing on graph paper first, number the squares, lay out the strips on pieces of mat board, and then put a number by each stack of strips.

I don't think I'd be trying these larger, more complex pieces if I hadn't made a few hundred small pieces, including the dozen or so that were so awful that I threw them out or gave them to the kids. The great drawing teacher, Kimon Nikolaides, said in *The Natural Way to Draw,* and I repeat to myself, "The sooner you make your first five thousand mistakes, the sooner you will be able to correct them." Seeing mistakes as educational, taking note of the problems, joyfully discarding the ill-made pieces, and getting on with the next thing is much easier when the investment is of days or hours, instead of months. In the same way, working in a series, as I do by working the same pattern over and over, lets you apply all that education to a similar work.

Buying and storing cloth

I started buying cloth long before I thought of making quilts from it. I hung around cloth stores, a color-hungry drawing and printmaking student (all that white paper and black ink!). Printmaking, being hard to interrupt and messy, fell by the wayside as soon as I had babies to care for. I still would rather spend time in a good cloth store than almost anywhere else, but I don't get to do that often. When I do, I buy a yard each of what I like best, looking out for needed or hard-to-find colors. Trying to design in the store isn't a good idea. The light is usually bad, the smell of preservatives is at least a bit of a bother, and the surroundings are cluttered and distracting. It's better to consider your cloth collection as a resource that needs constant replenishing. I buy mostly domestic cottons, which are getting more and more beautiful, and whatever I can afford of imported pimas—they're a little harder to control but have a wonderful sheen and delicacy. Once home, I wash and line-dry all the new cloth and iron those pieces that really need it.

My workshop in our old farmhouse is a large room with lots of natural light. I keep the white window shades down most of the time to cut the glare and minimize fading; the room isn't at all dark, but the light is diffuse. I store the cloth sorted by color in

Strip-piecing the "Trip Around the World" quilt

The "Trip Around the World" pattern is a mandala form, with concentric diamonds around a center square. It consists of four identical corner squares, four center strips, and a center square. These instructions are for a seven-square quilt, but you can make the pattern with any odd number of squares above three.

I usually start designing a small "Trip Around the World" quilt with one color or a few related colors. I stack the chosen fabrics in order; the series usually progresses from light to dark or from one color to another.

If the center portion of the quilt contrasts significantly with the corners, the piece will work best if the shift occurs at, or within, the last complete diamond (#4 fabric in example); otherwise, the eye will be drawn to the four corners. Similarly, any fabric that will be the focus of attention by virtue of its brilliant color or large-scale print should be within the diamond. Press open all seams after stitching.

1. Number the graph and arrange fabrics from 1 to 7. Cut the strips 1 in. wide and, for one seven-square quilt, 5½ in. long; this length allows 1½ in. for waste. You need one strip of #2 fabric, two strips of #3, three strips of #4, three strips of #5, two strips of #6, one strip of #7, plus a center square (#1).

2. Lay out the strips in groups as they'll be sewn together: 2, 3, 4; 3, 4, 5; 4, 5, 6; 5, 6, 7. Sew them together with ¼-in. seam allowances.

3. Cut each striped block crosswise into four strips of three fabrics each, discarding ¾ in. at each end. If you have no paper cutter, use a rotary cutter and a clear gridded ruler. Pile together the like strips and arrange them in ascending order: 2-3-4 strips, then 3-4-5 strips, and so on.

4. Sew together the strips, and the center square into blocks, as shown; then sew the blocks together in the order shown by the numbered arrows.

5. You can add four pieced sections to the sides: Sew together strips 7, 6, 5, 6, and 7 and strips 7, 6, and 7. Cut these strips, plus one #7 strip, crosswise into 1-in.-wide strips. Sew these together into four identical triangular sections, as shown. Sew to the center section. Trim to square the piece; add borders.

6. Sew on four 1-in.-wide strips for the border. Cut a backing square the same size as the bordered top. Pin the layers together.

7. Cut four 1½-in.-wide binding strips. Sew them, right sides together, to the top and backing. Turn under and pin the raw edges of the binding strips to the quilt back. Stitch the binding to the back. —S.S.

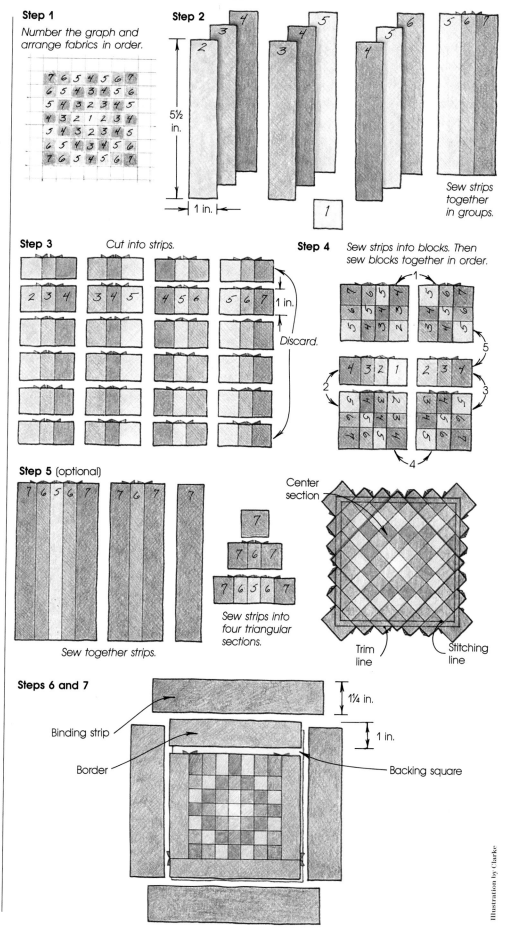

Step 1

Number the graph and arrange fabrics in order.

Step 2

5½ in.

1 in.

Sew strips together in groups.

Step 3 Cut into strips.

2 3 4   3 4 5   4 5 6   5 6 7

1 in.

Discard.

Step 4 Sew strips into blocks. Then sew blocks together in order.

Step 5 (optional)

7 6 5 6 7   7 6 7   7

Sew together strips.

7

7 6 7

7 6 5 6 7

Sew strips into four triangular sections.

Center section

Trim line

Stitching line

Steps 6 and 7

1¼ in.

1 in.

Binding strip

Border

Backing square

boxes in a glass-front bookcase. I cut out part of the fronts of the boxes so I can see the cloth inside, and I paint the insides with white latex paint to protect the cloth from acids in the cardboard.

Using prints

Printed fabrics with only two colors that don't contrast much with each other (or with more colors if they blend into each other) and a small pattern function almost as solids. From a distance the pattern isn't very noticeable; the surface is smooth. At the other end of the continuum are large-scale, high-contrast prints, a small piece of which will have indistinct edges, broken by color changes, and a coarse, visible texture. A pieced quilt made of small prints can look calm, orderly, precise; the same quilt in big or contrasting prints (photo, p. 10) will be active and complex, and the pattern of the squares will be hard to pick out. A combination of both in a quilt can be very interesting, as 19th-century quilts attest. I like prints that combine two very distinct colors; I use these fabrics as a bridge between fabrics in each of the two colors. This is another way in which you can make the pattern of the squares disappear.

I've always liked that quilts with printed fabrics contain the work not only of the quilt-makers but also of myriad anonymous fabric designers. I'm extremely particular about the prints that I purchase. If the artwork is good, I want the fabric; if it's boring or clumsy, I leave the fabric, though sometimes beautiful color can rescue a not-too-wonderful print.

Color

To me, color study is a lot like musical scales—it's something to practice and practice until it gets easy, and then practice some more. I consciously started to study color on my own during my first year at college, using Johannes Itten's *The Art of Color* (Van Nostrand Reinhold, 1974) as a guide. Itten combines color theory with an emphasis on getting the student to develop a personal approach to the use of color.

I've since seen some of Josef Albers' prints and used his fascinating and valuable book, *Interaction of Color* (Yale University Press, 1975), which is based on his many years of teaching at Yale. I believe what Albers said about there being no wrong colors, only colors in wrong proportions or combinations. I've also taken a color course with a

friend who paints on silk and teaches color theory. Finding people to talk to about color is helpful; taking a color course can help you build the habit and vocabulary for doing that. Color theory is important, and not very difficult, but it's just a lot of talk without practice. Albers says, "Knowledge and its application is not our aim; instead, it is flexible imagination, discovery, invention."

I'd take with a large grain of salt anybody's surefire system to make your colors work together, as the results may become too predictable and constraining. But one's own and others' observations of what's going on with colors are something else. I've trea-

"Trip Around the World," 1989, 7 in. x 7 in. (Photo by Len Mastri)

sured things I've picked up from people over the years. I've also collected postcards; magazine photos of nature, paintings, and quilts; my own colored-pencil drawings and gouache studies; scraps from quilts long gone and nearly forgotten; swatches that I like together; and anything that reminds me of what I've seen and liked.

I recommend keeping a notebook in which to save ideas and experiment. Use scraps of fabric and a glue stick or double-faced tape or colored paper collected from magazine pages or graphic designers' paper samples. Opaque watercolors—gouaches—in the primary and secondary colors and in black and white are easy to use on a heavy paper like Bristol board. Mark the paper with squares so you're not tempted to make a picture.

When I begin teaching a group of students, I tell them that each color is like a person, with a character, qualities, and messages, and that they can get acquainted

with a color faster by asking questions, such as: What color is it (hue)? Is it light, dark, or medium (value)? Is it pure, like a color in the rainbow, or mixed with black or white or gray (saturation)? Is it warm or cool or neither (temperature)?

A good color wheel is an invaluable aid; one made with paint by the student is best. Making pairs of colors is a way to begin learning about color relationships. Start with a favorite color. Combine it in equal amounts, like a four-patch, or as a figure and ground—with black; white; a gray of equal value; its complement; each of its neighbors on the color wheel; the same color with black added (shade), gray added (tone), white added (tint); the same color with some red-orange added to warm it up or blue-green added to cool it off; and so on. Then you could go through the same exercise with a color you hate and probably be surprised by the results. Along the way, you'll find pairs that resonate for you. Try to figure out what it is that you like about these color pairs. Also check out the preferences of the people around you.

Colors carry a lot of messages, so learning to use colors to say what we mean is important. In my classes, I have my students fill a 16-square grid with as many different colors as they want to express a mood or a season; for example, summer, early fall, late fall, winter, early spring, or late spring; and often, a pair of grids expressing opposing feelings: happy, sad; friendly, angry; soft, hard; bright, dull; quiet, noisy; young, old.

These grids won't be done the same way by any two people. I think of summer in Vermont as overwhelmingly green and blue, with flecks of bright flowers, but a group of fourth graders picked a jumble of bright reds, yellows, greens, blues, and oranges and achieved the active vividness of children's summertime just right.

Another interesting exercise is to make compositions in which all the colors share a given quality, such as pale, dark, warm, cool, brilliant, or neutral. Then see what happens when you add a touch of a color of the opposite quality to the composition.

It doesn't take much of this kind of purposeful play to start looking with new eyes at what's around and asking better questions when you're designing. □

Susan Sawyer makes quilts in her home in South Woodbury, VT.

Seminole Patchwork Deciphered

A primer on strip piecing

by Ginny Yund

When the hand-cranked sewing machine came to the Florida Everglades in the 1880s, the Seminole Indians began using it to embellish their clothing with colorful and ingenious patchwork bands. These designs were so small that it would have been impractical to piece them by hand. Instead, the Seminoles used a technique called strip piecing, machine-stitching strips of fabric into sets, then cutting the sets into segments and reassembling them to form the bands.

The Seminoles weren't the first people to use strip piecing, but the Seminole women developed the idea in such a distinctive way that the technique rightfully bears their name today. There are no early records of patterns that were created by the Seminole Indians. However, in 1980 a group of women, through the Seminole Research/Design Project, identified the basic band styles in their book, *Seminole Patchwork* (see "Further Reading," p. 17). Understanding these variations unlocks the possibilities of the technique. When I discovered their book, I was already teaching quilting, but I immediately plunged into strip piecing. Now I'm working almost exclusively in the technique and using variations of these basics.

Constructing the basic bands—There are six basic band styles (see drawings, p. 15). The methods of constructing each style are described below, but having to cut into fabric can be inhibiting when you're exploring new ideas, so I suggest that you start your explorations with construction paper and transparent tape. This way, you can ignore seam allowances, and you can quickly see if the strip sizes and proportions are appropriate for your project. When you want to convert to fabric, simply add ¼ in. to each seam edge for allowances.

If you do want to change the scale of a design, it's easy to do. Measure the finished size of the strips and segments. Then decide what you want the new scale to be (choose an easy multiple, perhaps one-half the size for a tie or three times the size for a

Giny Yund's wall quilt, "Seminole Spring," elaborates on traditional Seminole patterns by including stylized images of flowers (second band from bottom), but each band is still derived from one of the six basic band styles of Seminole strip piecing. This quilt uses styles #2 (made from 90°-cut segments of a simple strip set reassembled offset), #5 (made from segments from more than one strip set), and #6 (medallions made from segments from more than one strip set). From top to bottom, the styles (shown on p. 15) are: #2, #6, #5, #2, #5, #2, #5, #6.

From *Threads* magazine (October 1989) 25:39-43

Yund assembles quilts strip by strip, whether they're derived from Seminole designs or from traditional patchwork.

quilt), and multiply all your finished measurements by this factor. Then add the standard ¼ in. for each seam.

It's also a good idea, whether you're working in paper or fabric, to allow an extra ¼ in. on the top and bottom strips in a strip set to ensure that all of the design is accommodated when you apply the edging strips that usually finish off the top and bottom of band designs. I once spent hours making points meet in a chevron design, only to find that most of the points would be lost when the edging strips were applied.

First band style: This is the simplest band style to make. Segments are cut at 90° to the bottom of the set. Join two strips to form a strip set, pressing the seams carefully in one direction. Always straighten and square the end of the strip set from which you're going to work before you measure and cut the first segment. I begin at the left end. Periodically check to see that you're still cutting square. If not, square the end again before you cut any more segments. For this band style, you'll rejoin the segments side by side, reversing direction with alternate segments. Before you begin stitching, divide the segments into two stacks, reversing the segments in the second stack. Working in pairs, take a segment from each stack, put the segments right sides together, and place a pin where the seams join to hold them in place while you stitch. Once you've begun stitching the seam, you can remove the pin so you won't stitch over it. Press the seams in one direction after you've joined all the segments.

I always use ¼-in. seams for Seminole piecing and, as in traditional piecing, they're pressed to one side instead of open. It's best to work with pairs of segments, rather than continually adding new segments to a growing band. Place two segments right sides together and stitch ¼ in. from the edge. It isn't necessary to backstitch or tie threads. Feed pairs through the machine continuously without cutting threads between them; this is called chain stitching. When you've stitched all the pairs, cut the threads and start joining two sets of pairs. Continue like this until you've used all segments. You'll need a seam ripper, as it's easy to make a mistake with even the most careful planning. After you've joined all segments, press the seams in one direction.

The simplest of these designs results in a checkerboard pattern, but you can vary the design by using more than two strips and strips of different widths and colors. Edging strips can be wide or narrow, in proportion to the band. Or you might first use a narrow strip and border it with a wider one of a different color. Press the edging-strip seams toward the edging.

Second band style: Segments in this style are also cut at 90°, but they're rejoined offset or in stair-step fashion, and there are often at least three strips in the set. Sometimes the width of the central strip determines the amount of offset. I enjoy experimenting with the amount of offset to change the design. Notice that offset bands have slanted ends; the drawing at bottom left on the facing page shows how easy it is to straighten the ends without waste.

Third band style: Segments are cut at an angle other than 90° and are rejoined side by side. As with the first style, the direction is reversed with alternate segments. It takes practice to get the seams to meet precisely when you're rejoining the segments, as the seams will cross away from the edge when the segments are placed right sides together. You want them to cross exactly ¼ in. from the outside edge of the segments, so use a pin to find the cross and hold the segments in place while you're stitching. As with the first style, there won't be any waste at the top and bottom; the edging strips can be joined to the straight edge of the band. Before applying edgings, straighten the ends.

Fourth band style: Segments are also cut at an angle other than 90° but are rejoined offset, as in the second style. Again it's fun to experiment with the amount of offset. This band has slanted ends too, and you can straighten them, as shown in the drawing at right, before adding edging strips.

Fifth band style: Combination bands are composed of segments from more than one strip set. This idea is behind many of the most intriguing Seminole bands. The possibilities are endless. You can still chain-stitch if you organize the stacks of segments at the machine and plan the sequence of stitching. Don't stitch across a seam that hasn't been pressed, so you might need to assemble one group of segments and press all the units before going on to the next stage of construction. Remember to work in pairs of segments to keep the design flowing.

Sixth band style: Here, the main design is a medallion. Medallions usually require segments from more than one strip set. They can be used as isolated, single-design elements, or several can be joined to form a band. See "Strip-piecing Weaver's Delight" on p. 17 for more on isolated medallions.

Medallions in bands can be joined side by side, or they can be turned on point and joined with triangles. To make a band with medallions turned on point, measure one side of the finished medallion, add ½ in., and cut a strip of background fabric this width. Cut the strip into squares; then cut the squares in half diagonally to make right triangles, which you attach to opposite sides of each medallion (drawing at bottom right, facing page). Press seams toward the triangles and join all segments, pressing the segment seams in one direction. The hypotenuse of each triangle will be at the top and bottom of the band when the medallions are joined. Since this is the bias of the fabric, I staystitch across the top and bottom of the unfinished band if I'm going to handle it much before applying edging strips.

Beyond the basics—Even the most complex Seminole designs can usually be analyzed as variants of the basics. Knowing the principles of the technique allows you to create original designs and analyze a design that you're trying to reproduce.

Some projects call for bands that are mirror images of each other. For example, when arranging bands on a vest or jacket, you might want the bands to be symmetrical from the center front or back.

Mirror-image designs in bands where the segments are cut at a 90° angle are formed when the segments are rejoined. You offset segments down for one band, and up for the mirror image (see top drawing, p. 16). For bands with segments that are cut at an angle other than 90°, you create the mirror image when you cut the segments. Cut half of the segments slanting left to right, and cut the other half slanting right to left. Or, you can fold the strip set in half, wrong sides together, and cut through both layers at the same time, beginning at the fold.

Mirror-image bands can also be joined along their length to produce one wider band. Or right- and left-handed segments can be joined alternately to produce a chevron design (bottom drawing, p. 16).

At the top and bottom of my "Seminole Winter" wall hanging (photo, p. 16), I used a simple idea that's a variation of style three. I made a long strip set in which I arranged seven earth colors from dark to light. Then I cut the set apart with alternating oblique cuts to form triangles. I attached all the triangles with dark bases for the base of the piece, where I wanted some visual weight, and attached the remaining light-based triangles for the top band.

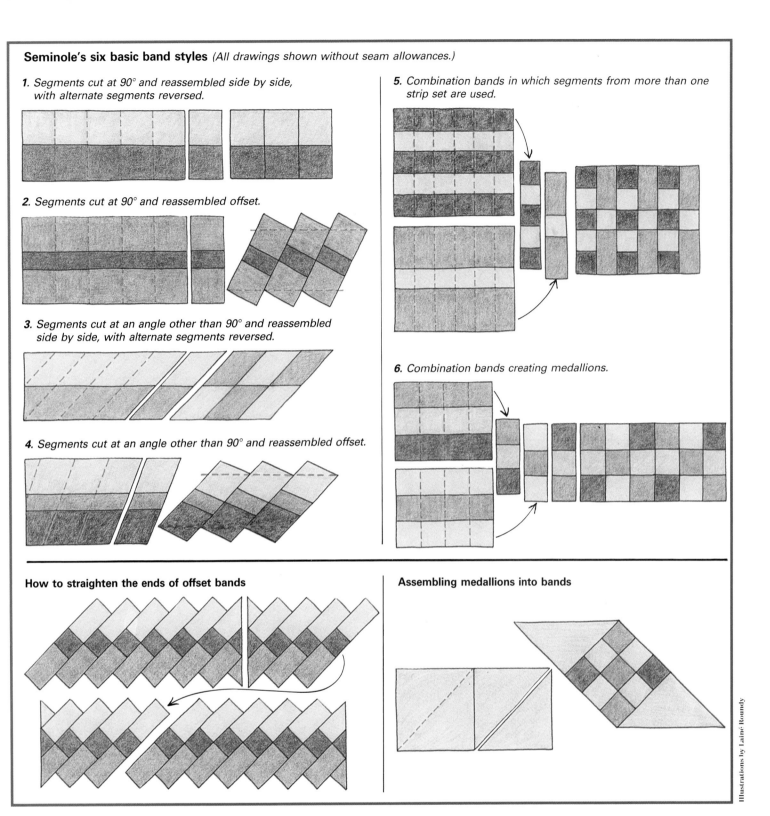

Seminole's six basic band styles *(All drawings shown without seam allowances.)*

1. Segments cut at 90° and reassembled side by side, with alternate segments reversed.

2. Segments cut at 90° and reassembled offset.

3. Segments cut at an angle other than 90° and reassembled side by side, with alternate segments reversed.

4. Segments cut at an angle other than 90° and reassembled offset.

5. Combination bands in which segments from more than one strip set are used.

6. Combination bands creating medallions.

How to straighten the ends of offset bands

Assembling medallions into bands

Illustrations by Lainé Roundy

Using color—The pleasure that I take in colors, whether I'm experimenting with them or just experiencing them, is an important influence in my life, and it's basic to my interest in strip piecing. Beautiful sunsets, fall foliage, flowers, and lush green meadows all give me a natural high, and the colors I use reflect my love of nature. Color, of course, can make all the difference in Seminole piecing. Traditionally, the Seminoles used strong colors—mainly reds, yellows, and blues. Their garments are highly distinctive and are bright and alive with color. The Seminoles rarely used patterned fabrics in the strips.

You can certainly use printed fabrics to advantage, but you should carefully consider how such fabrics will affect the design. A printed fabric placed in the central strip of a strip set can be very interesting, but if too many prints are used together, the design can get lost, and your careful piecing will thus be wasted. I've found it effective to use various values of the same solid color. I enjoy the subtle interactions and sense of movement that are created when you reverse the direction of alternate shaded segments. I also like the way that changing the color and placement of the edging strips can affect the design.

When I started working on "Seminole Winter," I had a problem with color. I'd chosen browns and neutral tones, black, white, sky blue, and the greens of conifers. But it wasn't coming together, and I removed the bright blue and greens. My first thought was, "I can't do this; it will be too dull." Then I remembered how I enjoy the neutral tones with black used by the Navajo in their beautiful woven rugs, specifically in the Two Gray Hills area, and I knew I couldn't go wrong. This wall hanging has become one of my favorites and confirmed for me the power of a limited color range.

(continued on p. 16)

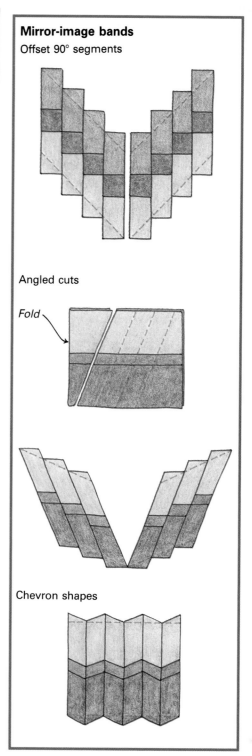

Mirror-image bands

Offset 90° segments

Angled cuts

Fold

Chevron shapes

Yund's "Seminole Winter" uses variations on the basic band styles of Seminole strip piecing. From top to bottom, the bands are derived from: styles #3, #2, #2, #5, #6, #2, #6, #3.

Some tricks for working with fabric—I prefer using fabrics that are 100% cotton because they're the easiest to work with. Cotton adheres to cotton, so you don't have the problem with slippage that you might have with other fabrics. Also, some blends have a tendency to ravel. When you use blends and cottons in the same project, you must set the iron temperature for the blend. Always prewash fabrics in order to avoid shrinkage after the piece is finished and to remove excess dye. It might be necessary to wash and rinse some solid colors several times until all the excess dye is out—rinse until the water is clear. Otherwise, your project could be ruined the first time you wash it. Even dry cleaning doesn't guarantee against colors running. After washing and drying fabric, I dampen it, roll it in a bath towel, and let it sit for several hours, just as was done with clothing years ago. When ironed, the fabric will be as smooth as when it came off the bolt.

Before beginning a project, clean and oil your sewing machine, and set the stitches at 8 to 10 per inch. If your machine doesn't have a presser foot that's ¼ in. from edge to needle, you should probably purchase one. Otherwise, you'll find yourself doing much more fabric marking than is necessary. A ¼-in. gauge on the base of your machine is some help, but any extended segments will make it impossible to rely on that as a seam guide.

In traditional piecing, you normally use an assortment of specialized templates to transfer piece shapes to your fabric. In Seminole piecing a gridded, plastic, see-through ruler is the only template you need. There are several very good ones available, which are marked off in ⅛-in. grids.

I use a rotary cutter against a ruler instead of scissors so I can cut strips and segments without marking the fabric. This is so fast and accurate that I wouldn't even consider using scissors to strip-piece anymore. Don't tear the strips, as some books suggest, and as the Seminoles no doubt did, because it's very difficult to measure accurately from frayed edges; and you have to measure, cut, and stitch accurately and

Strip-piecing Weaver's Delight

Once you've learned how to do Seminole piecing, you may want to look at traditionally pieced quilt patterns to see which ones you could piece by using a variation of this much-faster method. I recently pieced 54 blocks of "Patience Corner" (so named because of the patience required to piece it) in record time, using three strip sets. The more difficult block shown below, called Weaver's Delight, traditionally has 85 pieces in one 15-in. block. Instead of working with individual pieces, I sewed strip sets and cut segments. In fact, any design that can be gridded can be made with strip-piecing techniques, but if the design doesn't have a lot of repeated elements, it may not be worth the effort to figure out strip sets for it. —G.Y.

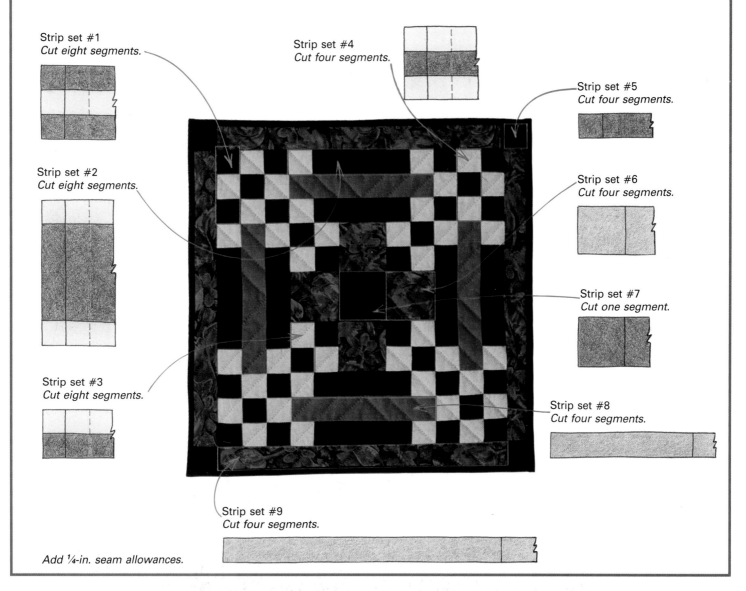

Strip set #1
Cut eight segments.

Strip set #2
Cut eight segments.

Strip set #3
Cut eight segments.

Strip set #4
Cut four segments.

Strip set #5
Cut four segments.

Strip set #6
Cut four segments.

Strip set #7
Cut one segment.

Strip set #8
Cut four segments.

Strip set #9
Cut four segments.

Add ¼-in. seam allowances.

press neatly to get nice definition in the design. It's important to cut on grain. I usually cut the strips on the straight grain of the fabric, parallel to the selvage, as the straight grain has very little stretch. When I'm reassembling the segments, I'm stitching on the cross grain, and its slight amount of stretch makes it easier to match the points. Some people like to cut strips on the cross grain so they can get 44-in.-wide strips from even ¼ yd. of fabric, but I usually purchase fabric in 1-yd. pieces or more and often work with strip sets of 1 yd. Don't cut strips or edgings on the bias.

The Seminoles don't quilt their piecework, but you might choose to do so, depending on the scale of the design. There are many seams to cross, so you must consider that when you decide where or how much to quilt. The larger the scale of the piecework, the easier it is to quilt—there's more space between seams. Try using a Seminole-pieced yoke on a quilted jacket or coat. If the pieced band isn't very wide, quilting along the edging strip will be sufficient, and you won't have to worry about quilting through all those seams. □

Ginny Yund has taught numerous courses and conducted workshops on quilting and Seminole piecing in Rhode Island. She is currently manager of The Spectrum of American Artists and Craftsmen, Inc., in the Providence Gallery.

Further reading

Barclay, Elaine, et al. *Seminole Patchwork: Principles and Designs,* 1980. Out of print, but available from Barbara Kahn, Box 1697, Boca Raton, Fl 33429 for $9.95 (includes S&H). *This book got me started; it's easy to follow and good for creating designs.*

Bradkin, Cheryl G. *The Seminole Patchwork Book.* Westminister, CA: Burdett Design Studios, 1980. *Has a useful glossary of patterns.*

Rush, Beverly, and Lassie Wittman. *The Complete Book of Seminole Patchwork,* 1982. Out of print, but available in libraries and used-book stores. *Has a nice selection of gridded patterns.*

Quilted Clothing

Get wearable results with thin batting and accurate piecing

by Mary Mashuta

Quilters have made quilted clothing for years, but currently the high-fashion world is showing great interest as well. If you didn't believe quilted fabric could be turned into clothing, now is a good time to give it a try.

Where do you begin? Actually, you start exactly where you would for many home sewing projects, by selecting a pattern and fabric. You can begin simply by embellishing just one area of a garment, such as a yoke or band, with patchwork. Or you can plan to piece and quilt an entire garment, like a vest. I'll discuss construction methods for both, along with some tips for accurate quilt-block drafting and piecing.

Finding a pattern

Quilting stitches, batting, and seams make a quilted garment stiffer than an unquilted one, so look for simple, dartless garments with minimum seams, such as vests, simple tops, and jumpers with plain bodices, like the one shown at right. Collarless jackets are also good. Sleeves with minimal ease in the cap combined with dropped shoulders translate best. Check out ethnic patterns, which often have panels and straight-sided pattern pieces, and patterns by designers such as Issey Miyake or Isaac Mizrahi. Folkwear patterns are good although sometimes you have to adjust their fullness.

Also consider closures when selecting a pattern. Buttonholes are difficult to make in quilted fabric, particularly if it is also pieced. Can you eliminate the buttonholes or substitute fabric loops? Can you fasten the shoulder of that jumper with large, flat pant hooks and eyes, rather than with buttons and buttonholes? Is it possible to close the garment with snaps and sew a button on top? Perhaps you could substitute a separating zipper for buttons and buttonholes, but be sure to adjust the pattern and remove the button lap.

Most quilted garments don't have facings; edges and seams are often bound with self-bias strips. The backing of the quilted fabric acts as a lining.

When you have found a likely pattern, make your fitting adjustments, then take the time to make a sample garment in muslin or leftover fabric. Trim the seam allowances from the neck, armholes of sleeveless garments, and opening edges of your muslin sample so it is easier to visualize where the edges are. Machine baste the pieces together, press, and try your sample on with the right side out, in front of a mirror. Evaluate the fit and do any fine-tuning that is necessary. Quilted garments aren't as drapable as standard garments; excess flare and fullness tend to translate into bulk. If possible, remove the excess or consider looking for another pattern.

Since pieced and quilted garments are bulkier and stiffer at the edges than standard garments, you may want to lower high necklines and drop the armhole depth for more wearing comfort.

Transfer any adjustments you have made to your tissue pattern, remembering to retain the seam allowances.

Selecting fabrics

It is possible to use many kinds of fabric for quilted garments. Firmly woven 100% cotton, like a broadcloth, or slightly heavier fabric is a good choice for a first project. Cotton/poly blends tend to stretch, which is why I prefer cottons. Silk is a nice fabric, but it's harder to work with than cotton. Heavier-weight silks such as noil are good possibilities.

It isn't necessary to limit yourself to quilter's calico. Stripes are one of my favorite patterns; the results often look much more complicated than they really are. By using very simple geometric shapes, you can create interesting, exciting designs. It's just a matter of learning to let the stripes work for you. For more on stripes, see pp. 20-21.

Batting

Most women don't want to look larger than they really are, so they shy away from quilted clothing. Quilted garments do not have to add inches. There are thin batts available designed specifically for clothing: Fairfield Processing's *Cotton Classic* (mainly cotton with some polyester), Mountain Mist's *Blue Ribbon All Cotton Batting,* and Hobbs' *Thermore* (polyester) are three such battings (see "Sources" on p. 22).

Another good batting is woven cotton flannel, which I've often used for my garments. Flannel adds little bulk and is cool even in warm weather. White or pastel colors won't show through your pieced fabric; check printed flannels for showthrough before you buy it as batting.

If you machine quilt the top only to the batting and not to the backing, smooth battings like 100% cotton, 80% cotton/20% polyester, or flannel work well because they don't catch in the feed dog. The batting texture is not critical if you quilt the layers to a backing fabric.

Accurate piecing

One of the main things to strive for in creating patchwork is to end up with quilt blocks or modules that are consistently the same size so they can be sewn together. To create accurate patchwork, you need to *accurately* draft blocks, add seam allowances to the individual pattern pieces, make templates, trace and cut out pattern pieces, and stitch seam allowances. This may sound complicated, but it actually makes the piecing process easier.

I draft and make my own patterns and

Piecing and quilting work best in garments with simple lines, like this jumper and vest. The jumper bodice is pieced with two different striped fabrics using Mary Mashuta's quilt block shown in the drawing on page 20. The neckband of the Issey Miyake vest is pieced with two fabrics. (Photo by Yvonne Taylor)

From *Threads* magazine (April 1991) 34:60-64

Stimulating stripes

Simple shapes can be cut from stripes and pieced to form interesting patterns. Using the same 3½-in. block, shown at right, I have created three very different patterns.

I like to use Japanese striped fabric, called *tsumugi* and *tosan*, but there are many striped fabrics suitable for patchwork. Guatemalan and decorator-weight fabrics are possibilities; if you use these heavier fabrics, keep individual pattern pieces as large as possible.

I categorize stripes as *even* or *uneven*. An even striped fabric, shown in the upper left photo on the facing page, will form a mirror image if folded along one of the stripes; an uneven fabric (upper right photo) will not. This is an important characteristic to keep in mind when deciding how to use the stripes in a block.

Stripes can be arranged parallel or perpendicular to the hypotenuse of my block's triangles, or parallel to one of the sides. When four blocks with similarly arranged stripes are grouped together (drawing at right), the stripes can form concentric squares, Xs, or windmill patterns.

A good way to start playing with stripes is to take several pieces of white paper and cut geometric openings the shape of your pattern pieces, in different sizes, and use the windows to preview fabric pieces. When you move the windows around on the fabric, you'll see only limited portions, giving you an idea of how each shape will look.

Use the template's registration marks to line up the stripes accurately. Remember to purchase additional fabric when you're piecing stripes.

If you're using many different striped fabrics in a complex design, it's easier to keep track of the pieces if you arrange them on a pin-up wall or tabletop, organized according to your design. For first projects, stitch the pieces together, block by block. Once you're comfortable working with stripes, you can streamline the process by sewing as many seams as possible at each sitting, "railroading" or "tandem piecing" short seams together in a single chain of stitching (photo, below).

Stripes make hand quilting difficult to see, so I machine quilt my striped-fabric garments. I use hand quilting only where it will show.—M. M.

Mashuta's optical block pattern

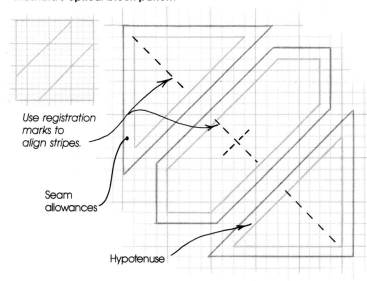

Use registration marks to align stripes.

Seam allowances

Hypotenuse

Stripe layout

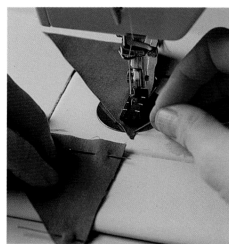

Stripes are perpendicular to hypotenuse.

Stripes are parallel to triangle side.

Stripes are parallel to hypotenuse.

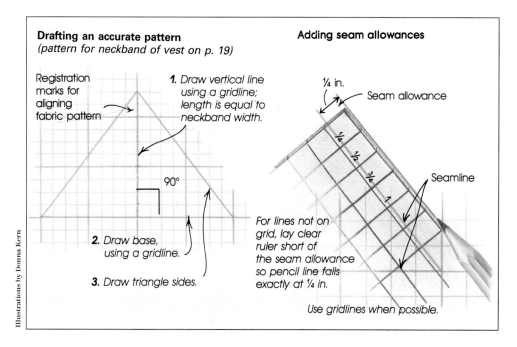

Drafting an accurate pattern
(pattern for neckband of vest on p. 19)

Registration marks for aligning fabric pattern

1. Draw vertical line using a gridline; length is equal to neckband width.

90°

2. Draw base, using a gridline.

3. Draw triangle sides.

Adding seam allowances

¼ in.

Seam allowance

¼

½

¾

1

Seamline

For lines not on grid, lay clear ruler short of the seam allowance so pencil line falls exactly at ¼ in.

Use gridlines when possible.

Illustrations by Donna Kern

The Little Foot makes it easy to sew accurately. The right edge is exactly ¼ in. away from the needle hole; the left, ⅛ in. Stitching groups of paired seams with a continuous line of stitching as shown is called "railroading."

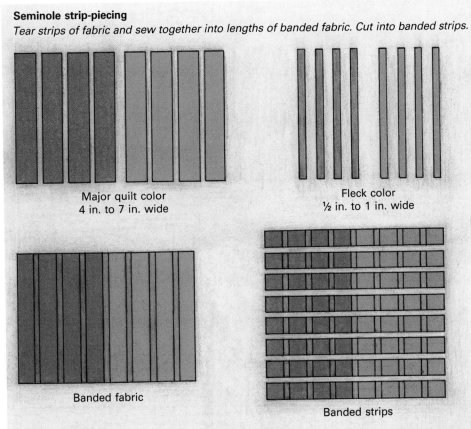

Seminole strip-piecing

Tear strips of fabric and sew together into lengths of banded fabric. Cut into banded strips.

Major quilt color
4 in. to 7 in. wide

Fleck color
½ in. to 1 in. wide

Banded fabric

Banded strips

Sketch of "Red Hot Red"

Sketch (not to scale) has a grid pattern of 1 in. = 1 ft. Letters represent major quilt pieces; numbers indicate blocks of parallel strips. Arrows indicate direction of quilting. Fine lines represent quilting guidelines.

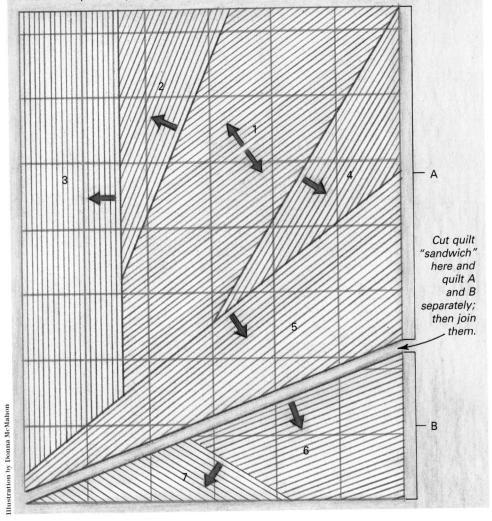

A

Cut quilt
"sandwich"
here and
quilt A
and B
separately;
then join
them.

B

Illustration by Donna McMahon

ing a rotary-blade cutter, a steel ruler, a T-square, and a cutting mat, I cut banded strips. I don't know exactly how much fabric I need, and sometimes I have a little bit left over.

Now I'm ready to decide on the small-scale color schemes in the quilt, where the light and dark areas of bands of color will fall. I lay the quilt sandwich on my worktable and arrange the strips of banded fabric on top of it. I pay attention to the rhythmic placement of the flecks of various colors. I offset the same color flecks and create dotted paths rather like musical notation on a staff line across the quilt. After I've decided on the arrangement, I keep the strips in order and ready for sewing.

Sewing order—The order of sewing all the fabric strips to the muslin fleece backing is critical to ensure that I don't sew myself into a corner. I look for ways to complete a block of parallel strips and to progress cleanly across the rest of the quilt without a break. Starting from the edge of a block whose edge is a complete strip or from the middle of a block, I work toward the opposite edge or outer edges, respectively (bottom drawing). If I start in the middle of a block, I can pin and then sew two strips at a time. If I've planned the sewing order correctly, the adjacent block will have a strip that runs across the entire edge of the first, which when sewn down, will cleanly finish the raw strip ends.

I start by pinning the first strip to a quilting guideline on the muslin with pins spaced every 2 in. Holding the roll of quilt, I machine-stitch one edge of the strip through all layers of the quilt; then I iron the seam from the right side. To stitch the second strip, I pin it with right sides together to the first strip and sew a ⅛-in. seam, again through all layers of the quilt. After I make each seam, I haul the quilt roll off my machine and iron the seam from the right side.

If the quilt has two pieces, I sew them by machine with right sides together. After grading the fleece, I iron the quilt and then cover the raw edges on the back with a casing. To finish a quilt, I square the piece and trim excess with the rotary cutter. I then add a narrow binding that I hem down to the back by hand.

After completing "T-5" (photo, p. 24), the first quilt in my "color-field" series, which was inspired by color-field artists like Marc Rothko and Jules Olitzki, I made four other quilts, all with hard-edge separations of color areas and flecks to break up the solid-color areas. Each quilt was minimal in composition but achieved a monumentality that satisfies my vision of color-field quilts.□

Judith Larzelere, whose article exploring variations on Log Cabin quilting appears on pp. 44-48, lives in Dedham, MA. Photos by Bindas Studio.

Amish Quiet, Amish Quilt
The plain and not-so-simple Nine Patch

by Sue Bender

do the objects we make reflect who we are and what we value? I've been wondering about that question ever since I walked into a clothing store twenty years ago and saw old Amish quilts used as a background for men's tweeds. At first glance the quilts looked simple. A few large geometric shapes—bars, diamonds and squares—and odd color combinations of deeply saturated dark material. The basic forms were tempered by tiny, in-

tricate black quilting stitches. Unassuming objects, calm and intense at the same time.

That summer was an exceptionally busy time for me as I prepared for a show of my ceramics. But trancelike, I found myself back at the store every day to stare at the quilts. Their spartan shapes sent shock waves through me; the connection was immediate and electric. Each time I looked at them, my usual busyness stopped and I felt calm. I kept trying to understand how pared down and daring could go together.

I had to know more about the life of the farm women who had made the quilts. Finally, I found a quilt dealer who lived among the Amish. "No one is labeled an artist in an Amish community," he said. "That would be considered a sign of false pride. Things were made to be used, not

When Sue Bender lived with the Amish, she was given these dolls and their quilt. Graven images are forbidden by the Bible, so doll faces are blank. (Photo by Sid Levine)

From *Threads* magazine (August 1990) 30:68-71

revered," he added. Every woman quilts and makes dolls for her children. No one is singled out. Ambition doesn't get in the way. Making a doll or a quilt like those at left and on p. 28 is no more special than canning green beans or baking a cake. An Amish mother isn't looking for recognition or searching for self-expression as her finger stuffs the doll with straw and she makes its clothing from her unneeded scraps. Her ego doesn't have to compete with the object; its utility, not the reflection of the maker, is the important thing.

How opposite I was from the Amish. I was proud to think of myself as an artist with a capital A. My life was like a Crazy Quilt. Getting ready for the ceramics show, I was tempted in all directions. Trying to make each piece more original than the next, the more I tried to force something fresh, the more I failed.

The source of Amish art

I decided to go live with an Amish family. Everyone laughed and said that no Amish family would have me, but after almost a year of searching, I found a minister's family that was willing to take me in.

When I walked into the farmhouse that was to be my home for the next seven weeks, I entered a world of immense inner quiet. I had never been in a home that felt like that. The room glowed. It went beyond everyday cleanliness and order. I usually walked around in an excited state, my mind racing, but after being in the kitchen for a few minutes, I slowed down and began to feel calm.

Everything was a ritual. Doing the dishes, mowing the lawn, baking bread, quilting, canning, hanging out the laundry, picking fresh produce, weeding. Emma, Lydia, and Miriam, three generations of women living side by side, knew exactly what had to be done and in what order. Nothing had to be explained. The

A special reminder of her first visit among the Amish, "Lydia's Square" was the result of Sue Bender's collaboration with her host family. (Photo by Sid Levine)

women moved through the day unhurried. There was no rushing to finish so they could get on to the "important things." For them, everything was important. No distinction was made between the sacred and the everyday. Five minutes in the early morning and five minutes in the evening were devoted to prayer. The rest of the day was spent living their beliefs. Their life was all one piece. It was all sacred—and all ordinary.

I was happy pitching in and feeling useful, but I hadn't learned how to relax and just be with the family. I wanted to do an art project, something that would be uniquely mine. I decided to make something connected to the Amish quilts, but I needed cotton and all I saw around me was polyester. For an Amish mother with twelve children, polyester is a godsend. It means no ironing. I asked if I could use some of their old clothing in my project. But they didn't know or trust me yet, so they said no.

I decided to walk to a town ten miles away to find the local general store, famous for its vast supply of solid-colored cotton fabrics. As I walked across the countryside, the Amish stared. I was the "peculiar" one. Families in buggies nodded, giving a half wave, acknowledging some relationship. Without telephones, everyone knew everyone else's business. By now the word was out: The Yoders had taken in a stranger from California.

"Am I on the right road?" I kept asking, unsure of my destination, literally, figuratively, on every level. On this hot summer day, the walk seemed to take forever. Buggy rides were offered, but I was determined to walk. The general store was my reward—bolt after bolt, row after row of splendid cotton colors. "It's no bother," they assured me, as they cut 25 one-eighth-of-a-yard pieces of material from 25 bolts. With a ten dollar bundle under my arm and some shoofly pie in my belly, I headed home.

"Would it be all right to work on the kitchen floor?" I felt brazen asking, and didn't want to intrude on their routine, but my room had no extra floor space and poor light.

"Can I help?" Lydia asked, as she saw me begin to cut out a pile of one-inch squares to make groups of nine-patches.

"Of course." I measured and she began to cut. Titus, her twelve-year-old cousin who had come over to help Eli with the chores, shyly asked if he could join in. "Of course."

As a designer, I am quite definite. I have strong opinions, and I don't care if others agree or not; but now, as the three of us worked, I asked Lydia and Titus if they wanted to design the project. That sounds easy enough, but letting someone else take charge was a big step for me. "You don't have to be in charge all the time," I had to reassure myself.

Lydia and Titus plunged in, choosing from the pile of colors. They worked separately, moving the squares around, arranging and rearranging. What emerged was a remarkable array of highly original color combinations, variations on the Nine Patch pattern. Lydia's eye was especially good. Where did she learn this?

"Maybe I can find some old dresses," Miriam offered, watching the flurry of excitement. "I can't use them for anything else, so if you like, we can cut them up." Hearing her say "we" sounded lovely. No longer suspicious, she returned with a bundle of old, very worn dresses. I had passed an unspoken test, and now her old clothes, a part of her history, could join my new patches.

Emma looked on, enjoying the pleasure the children were having, and especially my appreciation for Lydia's new-found talent. "Maybe I could sew them up for you on my machine," she said hesitantly. She had an old-fashioned treadle sewing machine.

To me, sewing the fragments had always made them feel contained and hemmed in, but I didn't want to interfere with the process. At that moment, Emma's wanting to be a part of what was happening was more important than my artistic prejudices. She stitched the pieces together and delighted in watching the nine-patches take shape.

Next it was Miriam's turn to offer her services. Decisions had to be made about size and proportions, and the relationship of the inner and outer borders. To be old is to be respected in this community, and Miriam, the senior member of our team, was clearly in charge. She knew the rules—and the rules were to be followed. "I'll put it on a frame and quilt it," she said.

By noon, the immaculate kitchen was a mess. I couldn't believe what I was seeing. I had turned an orderly household into a three-ring circus. What would happen if Eli came home for lunch and saw this? Timid Emma assured me that it would be all right.

The Amish don't want people to photograph them, but we had produced a "photograph" more vivid than any camera could have. This 6- x 9-inch Nine Patch quilt, "Lydia's Square," at lower left, hangs in my studio, a happy reminder of that day.

The impact of the Nine Patch

To try to understand more about Amish quilting and the Amish relationship to the Nine Patch, I read many books. See the list under "Further Reading" on p. 29 for the ones I found most illuminating. But nothing explained how or why these plain people were able to create an art form that is so powerful, that it has a lasting impact on us today.

I think the wonderful vitality of these quilts comes from a practicality; form and

A masterpiece of paradox, this Nine Patch variation's symmetry is broken and enhanced by its piecing. Elegant quilting contrasts the rectilinear shapes, and the inner border of quilted scallops completely frames the partial piecing. (Photo by Sharon Risedorph and Lynn Kellner, courtesy of the Esprit Quilt Collection)

function are one. Stripped down to the essential, this no-frills way of life, with its great spareness, allows for a different kind of freedom. Theirs is a culture based on humility; it is a way of life that allows the individual to get out of his or her own way. For me, the great strength of the Amish comes from their art being a part of their life. It is all of one piece. Since all work is important, all work is valued. They honor both the process and the product.

What I saw among the Amish was the amazing amount of energy available to people who get pleasure from what they are doing and find meaning in the work itself.

They understand that it's not rushing through tasks to achieve a series of goals that is satisfying; it's experiencing each moment along the way.

When I started this journey of the spirit, I hoped a new pattern would emerge to replace the Crazy Quilt of my life, but there was nothing I could willfully do to change it. I had never planned to write a book, but one day after many visits, I was churning butter and suddenly realized that there were no more questions I needed to ask. If there were any answers, they were inside me.

During the five years I wrote *Plain and Simple*, the image of the basic Nine Patch

stayed with me as I worked in the studio. Suddenly the Nine Patch became intensely personal. I was surprised and at first disappointed. How could the pattern of my life be so ordinary? Eventually, I realized that there is nothing simple about the Nine Patch, which belongs to both the Amish and the "English" worlds. (The Amish call all outsiders "English.") Its varieties, mutations, and possibilities are almost endless. Having limits, subtracting distractions, making a commitment to do what you do well, brings a new kind of intensity.

As I wrote, I began to see I was making a Nine Patch quilt of my life. Each patch grew out of something I had seen or felt when I lived with the Amish. Each patch showed me a new way to look at something I had taken for granted. Each patch made me question my assumptions about what goes into the making of a good life. When my ego got out of the way, my work had an inner light—something "beyond me."

The patches of my quilt (below) are strong and fragile, both. I'm not going to stitch them together. Nothing is fixed, and there is no right way for them to be. There are patches I'm still working on, not sure where they belong or if they belong. Some patches may clash, some may be missing, and there are probably more than nine. This quilt will tell my children something about my life and the things I came to value. The Amish keep the borders of their quilts closed. Mine must remain open. □

Sue Bender, of Berkeley, CA, wrote Plain and Simple: A Woman's Journey to the Amish, *1989 ($16.95, hardcover, Harper & Row, San Francisco, The Ice House, 151 Union St., San Francisco, CA 94111), after spending part of five summers living with Amish families in Iowa and Ohio. Parts of this article are drawn from it.*

Sue Bender's "Amish Squares #3," is a variation on the traditional Nine Patch, a pattern of infinite possibilities. The open, unstitched edges contrast with the borders that complete Amish quilts. (Photo by Sid Levine)

Further Reading

Bishop, Robert, and Elizabeth Safanda. *A Gallery of Amish Quilts: Design Diversity from a Plain People.* New York: E.P. Dutton, 1976.

Granick, Eve Wheatcroft. *The Amish Quilt.* Intercourse, PA: Good Books, 1989.

Hostetler, John A. *Amish Society,* rev. 3rd ed. Baltimore, MD: Johns Hopkins University Press, 1980.

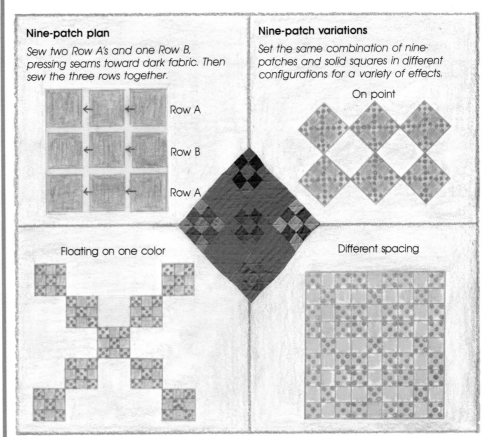

Nine-patch plan

Sew two Row A's and one Row B, pressing seams toward dark fabric. Then sew the three rows together.

Row A

Row B

Row A

Nine-patch variations

Set the same combination of nine-patches and solid squares in different configurations for a variety of effects.

On point

Floating on one color

Different spacing

For a Double Nine Patch, five small nine-patches are individual squares in larger nine-patch units set on point. (Photo by Sharon Risedorph and Lynn Kellner, courtesy of the Esprit Quilt Collection)

Making a Nine Patch

by Sondra Kennedy

The Nine Patch is a simple, basic patchwork pattern, reflected in many everyday things—a checkerboard, a tile floor, tic-tac-toe boxes. Young Amish girls usually learn to piece on a Nine Patch, and often make doll quilts with the pattern. However, the Nine Patch is not limited to the Amish—it appears in quilts across the United States. It can be used in a simple, homey quilt made with scraps, or in a sophisticated graphic statement worthy of a museum wall.

Nine-patch construction is simple: Cut five dark squares of fabric and four light ones, all the same size (or four dark and five light). Sew two rows of three patches, dark, light, dark; and sew one row of three patches, light, dark, light, as shown in the drawing at upper left. Use ¼ in. seams; press seams toward dark fabric; and press each row separately. Then sew the three rows together to form a nine-patch.

A design made of nine-patches can be changed by simply turning the squares of patches on point, changing the amount of space between the nine-patches, enclosing them with bands of color, or letting them "float" on one of their colors. Add to this the manipulations of

color, and the possibilities are endless, as suggested in the drawings above.

Amish women have few creative outlets. Their homes are simple, utilitarian, unadorned, much like their clothing. Their flower gardens, however, are often a riot of color. Gardening and quiltmaking are areas where it is acceptable for these "plain" women to let their creative juices flow. The simple Nine Patch is perfect for extraordinarily creative quilts from plain beginnings as, shown in the photos at left and above. In addition to using lovely, often unusual solid colors in their quilts, the Amishem ebellish them with beautifully designed, magnificent quilting—sometimes 20 stitches to the inch. Feathered wreaths, flowers, hearts, cables, and leaves are just a few of the quilting designs. They use black quilting thread, which makes the designs seem to melt into the fabric and at the same time provides a textural contrast to the geometric patchwork. Harmony between the patchwork pattern and the quilting itself is important, and the fine Amish quilts reflect this. □

Sondra Kennedy of Berkely, CA, wishes she could quilt all the time.

Medallion Quilting

A carefree way to quilt, building the design as you sew

by Kristin Miller

Only recently have we gotten the idea that we need a set of detailed, printed instructions before we can create a patchwork design. Two hundred years ago, women made quilts without the plastic see-through templates, graph paper, marking pens, and quilt-magazine patterns that we take for granted. Our great-grandmothers copied and exchanged patterns by closely observing one another's work, sketching an admired design, or making up a sample block out of fabric, with very little designing, planning, or measuring.

Many early quilts in North America were medallion quilts. A medallion quilt is constructed concentrically from squares and triangles arranged in one border after another. It does not need to be planned; design decisions can be made as new borders are sewn on. This encourages both frugality and imagination. Although new yard goods are sometimes used, more often scraps and remnants are added as they become available. If the widths of the borders are suitably varied, the pieces can be made to fit without precise measuring. As new patchwork motifs are discovered or created, they can be incorporated into a new border.

It is easy to imagine the medallion-quilt-maker playing with her fabric scraps long ago, deciding as she sewed what to add next. Perhaps she had a paper or tin template to measure the center squares, but the triangles were often random in size.

How medallion patchwork is built—When you are making medallion patchwork, you don't need to plan the pattern or the colors; you don't even need to visualize the finished quilt. You simply make a number of small decisions as your quilt progresses.

Starting with a center square, you choose fabrics for triangles to sew onto each side. Then you decide on the fabrics for triangles to sew onto the other two sides, and so forth, as shown in the drawing on the facing page. Choose each border by eye, holding different fabrics up to your growing

medallion and picking the one that looks best. When you want to get fancy, you can construct more elaborate patchwork borders by combining smaller patchwork units.

Your quilt grows larger as it grows outward in a series of concentric borders. How do you know when it's finished? When it's big enough, when the design seems complete, or when you get tired of working on it. If it isn't large enough for its intended purpose, finish it off with a broad outer border.

There is no need to be timid when you choose fabric for a quilt. Bold patterns and colors add life and interest to your design. Gather together fabric that you like. Don't worry whether the pieces match or go to-

gether. You'll probably have small bits of some fabrics and large amounts of others.

You'll also need these basic tools: scissors, an iron (to press the fabric before you mark or cut it), needle and thread, a sewing machine (optional—sewing by hand is fine too), pins, felt markers, pens or chalk, measuring tools, and templates. A padded table that can be ironed upon makes an ideal work surface.

Marking and cutting—There are various ways to mark accurate triangles. Stationery and school-supply stores sell plastic triangles in a variety of sizes. These right-angled 45° triangles are inexpensive, per-

Many 18th- and 19th-century quilts were made without patterns or templates. This mid-19th-century "Central Square in a Diamond," of handspun and handwoven wool, is composed of squares and triangles. Kristin Miller's simple border-by-border quilting method produces this type of central-medallion patchwork design. (Photo courtesy National Museums of Canada, Canadian Museum of Civilization, neg. #S79-4315)

haps $.50 or $1 apiece, and well worth having in several sizes.

You can make templates out of cardboard. Start by making a perfect square out of two same-size rectangular pieces of lightweight cardboard, such as two index cards or the cards from packages of seam binding. Lay the rectangles at right angles to each other, lining up their common corner and edges. Using the top card as a ruler, draw a line across the bottom card. You can then divide this square diagonally and cut it into two triangles. It is important to be very accurate in making templates.

You'll need four fabric triangles for the first border. A felt pen or tailor's chalk can be used to mark around the template. Line up the triangles so they share a common cutting line.

How big should the triangles be? As you'll see, there is no right or wrong size. The size depends on the effect you want and the amount of fabric you have to work with. Measurements don't need to be terribly precise. If the long side of the triangle is about ½ in. longer than the side of the square, a ¼-in. seam allowance will take up the extra amount and create an exact fit.

If you're a perfectionist, you'll probably try hard to get a precise fit. If you don't care that much about being perfect, you'll find it much easier, and just as satisfying, to make a good guess and use whatever triangle seems to fit. It's a lot less bother, and the results will still be pleasing.

Sewing and deciding—Start your medallion with a square. Lay the first triangle along one side of the square, lining it up so the same amount sticks out on either corner. Good sides of the fabrics should face each other. Pin them perpendicular to the seam, or iron the two pieces so they stick together by means of static electricity.

Use a ¼-in. seam allowance. Most presser feet measure ¼ in. from the needle to the outside edge of the foot and can be used to guide your sewing by keeping the edge of the presser foot running alongside the edge of your fabric. Sew slowly if you have trouble maintaining a straight seam. Press the seam flat from the front. Throughout the entire process, press each seam as you sew it so everything stays smooth and flat.

Position, sew, and press the second triangle the same as you did the first, but on the opposite side of the square. Follow the same process for the third and fourth triangles. The little "ears" sticking out will be covered by the next border.

You get a different effect with different-size triangles. Larger triangles will give a broader border. Sew the first two triangles as usual; then press them. Line up the third triangle with the third edge of the square. The ears of the first triangles will stick out (top-left drawing, page 33). Sew the usual ¼-in. seam all along the long edge of the triangle, clip off the ears, and press. Repeat on the fourth edge. ⟹

Building a medallion quilt

1. Begin with a square. Placing right sides together, sew on two triangles.

2. Sew on two more triangles.

3. Sew on two strips.

4. Sew on two longer strips.

5. Sew on another set of four triangles.

6. Sew on another set of four strips and continue until quilt top is as big as you wish. The strips can be triangles sewn together, or they can be plain or patterned cloth.

Miller (left) sews the final border strips on her medallion quilt. The back of the patchwork medallion (above) seems messy compared with the front, but it doesn't matter, as long as all the seams are sound. (Photos by Nancy Robertson)

Smaller triangles will give another effect. Center the four small triangles on the sides of the square and sew them on. Press. As you can see in the middle drawing on the facing page, the triangles don't reach clear to the corners of the square. When the next border is added, the corners of the inner square will be cut off, creating an octagon instead of a square in the center, and the four triangles will be isolated from one another.

Adding borders—To give a more complex design to the next set of triangles, I use highly patterned fabric like geometric and border prints. Lines that are part of a border-print fabric can create a frame for the inner medallion.

Add the second border of triangles as you did the first. When all four are sewn and pressed, you'll have a new and larger square, but tilted 90° to form a diamond.

You can make the next border of strips. If your previous border was somewhat uneven, bring the strip in toward the center so that you have a ¼-in. seam allowance all along. You can trim off extra fabric later.

To make strips, you can rip most fabrics, which gives a straight and accurate line. Just clip the edge and rip. Some synthetic fabrics don't rip well, so mark them with a felt pen or chalk, using a yardstick as a guide. Then cut them with scissors.

Sew and press two opposing strips, then the other two. Trim off any extra length, and give everything a good ironing.

The next border can again be made of strips; these can be fancy strips composed of many small triangles or squares in contrasting fabrics. Cut out some triangles and take a few minutes to arrange them in different patterns around your medallions. Then decide which arrangement you like best and sew it together.

To make a fancy border like the one shown in the top-right drawing on the facing page, sew triangles together along their long edges, using a ¼-in. seam allowance to make squares. After you press, snip off the little ears that stick out. Then sew the two-part squares into strips, matching the points carefully.

How many triangles do you need, and how big should they be? You can guess or measure, depending on how precise you like to be. If you guess, you'll probably make a number of squares and lay them out around the medallion—remember that the squares will become smaller when sewn because of the ¼-in. seam allowances on each side. Then sew the squares into strips, and see if they fit.

If the strips are a bit too short, trim a little off the four sides of the medallion. If the fancy strips are too long, you can enlarge the center medallion with a narrow strip. You can also vary the proportions of the patchwork border by changing the size and number of the triangles.

Adjusting the seams is another way to deal with fancy strips that are slightly too long or too short. If they're too short, rip out a few seams between squares and resew them with a slightly narrower seam allowance. If they're too long, take in the excess by resewing the seam allowances a tiny bit wider. Don't take out the first seam; just sew next to it. You can also make slight changes in the length of the strip by gently stretching to lengthen it or by shrinking it with a steam iron.

Lay the patchwork strip along the edge of the medallion, right sides together. Pin to hold it while you sew the seam. Sew the first two fancy strips to opposite sides of the medallion.

The remaining strips will have to be longer than the first two. You can add plain or two-part squares at the corners. When you are matching up the corners, it pays to be very careful because this is where it will be most noticeable if the seams don't match precisely. Pin exactly through the two seams to align them.

Iron the growing medallion, and pause to admire your creation. If you've gotten this far, you have mastered the basic skills of medallion patchwork. Now, should you make your next border out of triangles, strips, or fancy patchwork? □

Kristin Miller lives and quilts in Prince Rupert, BC, Canada.

Miller's finished quilt (right) is composed of concentric squares built up out of triangles and strips. It was made without any preplanning or measuring. (Photo by Julie Moore)

Using large triangles for a broad border

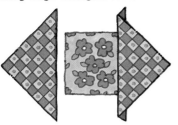

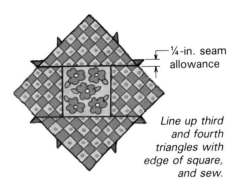

Begin with a square and two large triangles.

¼-in. seam allowance

Line up third and fourth triangles with edge of square, and sew.

Using small triangles to make an octagon

Center triangles and sew to square.

When next border is added, corners of inner square are cut off.

Fancy border strips

Make up strips of contrasting colored triangles.

Illustrations by Lainé Roundy

"Cut It Down the Middle and Send It to the Other Side"

Improvisational technique in African-American quilts

by Eli Leon

mprovisation is a vital and enduring force in African-American culture. It has its roots in African values that favor individuality and creativity. Improvisational variation in cultural forms ranging from music and dance to textile design is pervasive throughout black Africa, and it is also a prominent characteristic of African-American quilts.

Although African textile artists and African-American quiltmakers use traditional patterns and styles for their work, they retain the freedom to improvise. Accordingly, African-American quiltmakers are comfortable allowing new forms to occur spontaneously as an expression of underlying values that foster the salvaging of material and favor variation. Having this habit of mind encourages the unexpected, the unique, the personal. Quiltmaker Sherry Byrd describes herself as a person who is unable to stick with a pattern: "I don't like to use patterns. I think more so they're a waste of my time because it's *other people's ideas,* and not that I don't use other people's ideas, but, you know, I don't like to do the same things over and over, and so I just kind of build my own quilts as I sit at the machine."

Arbie Williams constructed her "Star and Wheel" quilt (76 in. x 67 in.), facing page, from rummage-sale patchwork finds and leftovers from her own piecing. Williams comfortably improvises to accommodate to the materials that she has at hand. Quilted by Irene Bankhead.

Delight in the unplanned – The knowledge of how African and African-American cultures manage the accidental and incidental is one key to understanding their improvisational processes. African textilemakers may *allow* for chance variations. Appliqué work on ceremonial skirts by the Kuba of Kongo, for example, serves to cover up tears as well as to decorate. Obviously, holes aren't planned; conversion to decoration depends on the embroiderer's flexibility.

African-American quiltmakers also enjoy the unplanned. Some work almost exclusively from scraps. Sherry Byrd says she gets her ideas from "the way the scraps are cut...you can just take them and start sewing with what's *there.*" Some, like Wanda Jones, favor scraps over new material. "If you got lots of big pieces of material," says Jones, "it's really not exciting to patch up anything. Quilting is making something good out of nothing. Then you can make something big out of something that's throwed away. That's what scrapping is all about. And you can make something beautiful out of scrapping."

Gussie Wells also likes scraps: "I prefer to use what the people give me because they has a whole lot of different kinds of material. They give you a whole lot of different pieces you would never bought." Her "Compound Strip" (left photo, below) is made from unusual fabric that was discarded by a windbreaker factory.

Although black quiltmaking emerged in a context of poverty, where recycling cloth made good sense, the exhilarating quilts crafted by African-Americans result from a dovetailing of economic and aesthetic considerations.

"Accidentals" are also embraced in African-American patchwork; piecing is seen as a process in which interesting things

Gussie Wells

can happen that aren't entirely controlled by the quiltmaker. "Mistakes" may be acceptable, or, not seen as mistakes at all, they may be welcomed as an integral part of the creative process (see Charles Cater's "Triangle Strip," below, right). According to Wanda Jones, when she was learning to

Charles Cater

quilt and would make a mistake, her mother would say, "It's nothing about making it a little different. It's still the same pattern. You just added something of your own to it." ⇒

Gussie Wells's "Compound Strip" (86 in. x 88 in.), pieced from scraps discarded by a windbreaker factory, is a sophisticated example of Afro-traditional strip quilting. Quilted by Willia Ette Graham.

Charles Cater has been making quilts for more than 50 years. In his "Triangle Strip" (98 in. x 88 in.), he has integrated an "accidental." Insetting the long vertical piece (upper-left area of central section) has enabled him to compensate for the narrowing strip. He highlighted the idiosyncrasy by using the light-colored fabric for the inset. Quilted by Willia Ette Graham.

From *Threads* magazine (October 1988) 19:70-75

Because the pieces in the "Basket Improvisation" quilt (77 in. x 89 in.) are unmeasured, the blocks vary in size, and alterations were necessary to fit them together. Note the range of orange forms that occur in the corners where four blocks meet.

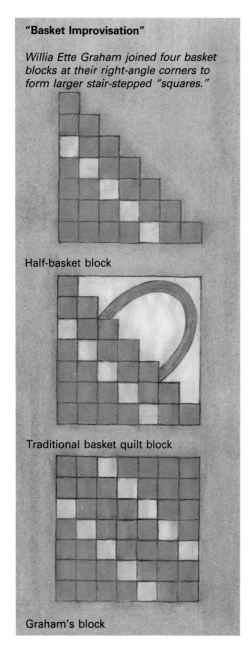

Half-basket block

Traditional basket quilt block

Graham's block

Willia Ette Graham

Willia Ette Graham used a modified basket block for the pattern in her "Basket Improvisation." She got the partial block (see drawing at top left) from a friend back home in Henderson, TX, in the 1960s. Ordinarily, it would be squared off with a solid-color fabric on which a handle for the "basket" would be appliquéd (center drawing). Instead, Graham made her unique block by piecing together two unfinished baskets. Though she often measures, she is adept at working with unmeasured pieces. For this quilt, Graham used precut scraps that were not uniform in size and, consequently, had to deal with a variety of tricky piecing situations. When four blocks left an empty space as they "met," Graham just filled in with the orange fabric that she had used to make the original blocks. She appreciates the unexpected: "When I get it together, well, I'm surprised at the quilt that I have made. It's so much different to what it's supposed to have been. It's a new pattern."

In African-American quiltmaking, improvisation occurs in a context of traditional restrictions. The artist works within prescribed boundaries that both regulate and yield to the creative process. The acceptance of incidental changes as creative offerings (unlikely in the Anglo tradition) affirms an innovative process that originates beyond the conscious domain and is basic to improvisation.

Arbie Williams

Arbie Williams (see her quilt on p. 34) also is not necessarily dissatisfied when she is piecing one of her quilts and a patch goes in differently than she'd planned: "Sometimes I really would like it, the way it come out. Sometime your ideals runs and then if you do it backwards, well sometime it fit in better than the way you had your ideals to go. So you just leave it like that…. it's different from anybody else's—so that's what you piece for, something different from somebody else."

Approximate measurement, antithetical to Anglo-traditional values as expressed in the standard patchwork quilt, is central to Afro-traditional aesthetics. Rosie Lee Tompkins (her quilt is shown on p. 38) doesn't do formal measuring when cutting out pieces for a quilt. Nor does Angelia Tobias: "No…I just cut them. Just long as they look right, I'll fit them. I just see that it'll fit in a certain design and just make it to fit." Tobias' grandmother, from whom she learned to quilt, didn't measure her pieces either. "I think she mostly just make everything by what she feel."

Charles Cater sometimes uses one piece as a template for the next, but, "Once you cut one piece…most of the time you use your own imagination from there on, and you can mostly come out just about the same…you cut and then you fit them in. You might have to trim…but that's about all." As for his teacher, his grandmother: "She would see something and she would just cut her pieces—start off from scratch with nothing and go on to make whatsonever she designed to do…whatsonever she feel like she want to make it out to be…I never see her measure anything."

Gussie Wells usually uses templates that she makes out of newspaper, but to cut straight pieces, "You just figure out how wide you want it and how long you want it, you just go whacking on it."

Sherry Byrd

Sherry Byrd sometimes measures precisely, but she believes that such measuring has its price: "I really don't like to sit down and do all that measuring. It just takes the heart out of things." She often chooses not to: "I just kind of eye things. Just see *how* I want it to go together and then put it together."

These cutting practices must be backed up by the skills necessary to deal with pieces that do not fit together. Byrd knows how to use variable-sized pieces. "When I sew them …together, there's just whatever size comes out. I just like to kind of put it together and look at it, and then if I need to go back and do a little trimming, I'll do that." Her "Double Medallion" (photo, facing page) sparkles with a lively irregularity. Tobias and Cater also say that they make the pieces fit or trim them. Uneven cutting is acceptable because the resulting variation is valued.

It is important that some of these freehand quilters remember that their mothers and grandmothers also worked without templates. Some of their grandmothers were young adults at Emancipation. The traditions of approximately measured piecing and accommodation for accidental variations may well stem from African-American slave culture and ultimately from African culture.

Improvisational patterns—It is likely that African women in the New World, approaching the piecing of a quilt block, had skills and attitudes about "accidentals" that allowed them an alternative to measuring. Unlike some Europeans, whom they may have seen measuring quilt pieces, they were adept at working from a "model in the mind."

The simplest forms of the improvisational block—blocks that use unmeasured pieces—are the String and the Crazy (three right drawings, p. 38). Both these forms are used by Anglo-traditional and Afro-traditional quiltmakers, but String quilts, where scraps of fabric of different lengths may be utilized by diagonal stripping, are especially popular in the black tradition, partly because they make such efficient use of the material. Willia Ette Graham uses her scraps as she finds them for some of her string quilts. "You don't have to cut for a string quilt. You just take those pieces whichever way they are."

The use of more complex improvisational blocks presents the quiltmaker with a succession of unforeseen predicaments. Managing difficult piecing situations calls for skills not required in the Anglo tradition and brings a second level of improvisation into play. If the Anglo-traditional quilt is properly executed, its final appearance is largely predetermined by the choice of pattern and fabric. The quiltmaker cuts and sews the pieces correctly to make consistent blocks and relatively predictable quilts.

Using approximate measurement, Afro-traditional quiltmakers must make continual adjustments as they fit the pieces together, since each block may be different in size or shape. Having to deal with such irregularities allows them to explore and excel in improvisational approaches that the Anglo-traditional quiltmaker is unlikely even to consider. The combination of approximate measurement, attitudes favoring elaboration, and a reliance on models held in memory thus ensures a high degree of variation.

Flexible patterning—In contrast to the single-fixed-motif approach used in Anglo-traditional patterns, the improvisational pattern is conceived of as a *range* of possible structures. It won't "repeat," but it will materialize as a sequence of visual elaborations. The quilt-artist can shift or modify the design at each rendition.

In Rosie Lee Tompkins' "Framed Improvisational Block" quilt (photo, p. 38), the flexible pattern is more elaborate than in most String quilts. Here, the prototypic block is composed of strips of squares in a frame. The squares may be further divided on the diagonal into Tents of Armageddon units (second drawing, p. 38), or they may be elongated into rectangles. Both between blocks and within particular blocks, the strips of squares may vary in size. The pieced strips may or may not be separated by un-

pieced strips. There may be from one to nine strips to a block. Two or more similar blocks may be assembled to form a larger unit. The frames may be wide or narrow, or an individual frame may vary in width. Three-sided frames are also an option.

Since Anglo-traditional quiltmakers limited structural variation within the block to the Crazy quilt (last drawing, p. 38) improvisational African-American quilts are often wrongly classified as Crazies by people who have no other category for them. Although Tompkins' flexible patterns are outside the confines of the standard American quilt tradition, they are ordered. Tompkins doesn't view the quilt block as an object to be repeated exactly, but as an invitation to variation.

African-American flexible patterning isn't limited to the quilt block. Gussie Wells has improvised a whole-quilt pattern in her "Compound Strip" (left photo, p. 35), taking off on the traditional African-American whole-quilt strip arrangement, wherein wider pieced strips alternate with narrower unpieced ones. Wells alternates wide and nar-

row strips, but all are pieced, and her sequence is more complex than the elementary aBaBaBa. She groups together ("compounds") similar strips and handles the whole-quilt pattern with the same flexibility that she might apply to a block pattern.

Restructuring—Restructuring is another Afro-traditional improvisational technique in which a pieced block or an entire quilt top may be cut up and put back together in a new way. It allows the quiltmaker to redo an overall design; use leftover, found, or inherited patchwork; or assemble a quilt top from variable-sized blocks. If a block doesn't fit a particular space, it may be cut down or built up. Cut-off pieces may be reshaped to fill in other odd spaces.

I became aware of it one day while talking to Angelia Tobias. She used to keep quilt tops on hand so that her customers could pick out the top they wanted her to make up for them. As we were going through them, she pointed out one that wasn't finished (top photo, p. 39). She

Sherry Byrd cuts off her pieced strips wherever necessary to fit them in place. As a result, her "Double Medallion" (74 in. x 86 in.) contains an assortment of unrepeated but related forms. Quilted by Irene Bankhead.

Some block forms

Ann and Andy
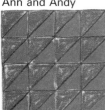

Tents of Armageddon
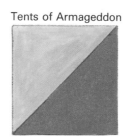

String
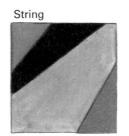

String

Crazy

The blocks in Rosie Lee Tompkins' "Framed Improvisational Block" quilt (74 in. x 86 in.) are not uniform in size or shape. Fitting them together, Tompkins finds additional opportunities to improvise. Her piecing techniques must be executed by hand; jigsaw-puzzle pieces cannot be set in place on a machine. Quilted by Willia Ette Graham.

planned to cut a section off one side and move it to the other to make it look better (lower-left photo). Once I had the concept, I could pick out other parts that had been cut after assembly.

Charles Cater has also restructured quilt tops. "You *look* at it, and you get a design of where your pattern should go and everything. And if you can, take part of that, cut it and take and put it in a different direction. It'll make that quilt much different that way. It'll make it show up better and make a beautiful quilt. So that's the way people done things when they has what you call a 'creative mind.' "

Sherry Byrd was enthusiastic about restructuring and liked having a word for something she said she did all the time. "Lots of times things get off balance...you're making a quilt and you look at it and it just doesn't seem right.... I always spread it out on the floor so I can see the whole thing." Her "Double Medallion" (photo, p. 37) includes a restructured block. Originally she had three of the medallion blocks. She sliced up the third block and fit the strips into one of the inner borders.

Arbie Williams also restructures: "If you get discomfortable with something you're making and you think it need to be on the other side, well just cut it down the middle and send it to the other side, or put it at the foot, wherever it look better." She also likes to use already-made patchwork. She can make use of whatever she comes upon because, as a skilled designer, well-versed in restructuring techniques, she comfortably improvises to accommodate to the materials at hand.

In her "Star and Wheel" (photo, p. 34), Williams has combined patchwork from three sources with some of her own. She used the corner wheels just as she found them. The central star originally consisted of five oversized sections that didn't quite meet to form a star but left too little room for the usual sixth point. She redid this star, making seven smaller sections out of the initial five and an eighth out of leftovers from a star quilt of her own. The four triangular sections of diamond patchwork are from yet another star she'd found unfinished years before at a rummage sale and had set aside until the right opportunity to use it came along. She cut this star into four parts and fit them in, adding fragments trimmed from the central star to bring them up to size. Finally, she added a pair of diamond border strips, using every bit of leftover patchwork from the first two stars.

Identifying Afro-traditional quilts—Some older Afro-traditional quilts are showing up anonymously, like the 19th-century Improvisational "Strip" (right photo, below). It seems likely that the quiltmaker used leftover blocks from several other tops (Log Cabin, Nine Patch, Dutch Tile, and Ann and Andy, the pattern used on the reverse of the quilt) because all the patterned blocks are either too wide or too narrow for the strip width. Oversized blocks are cut down; undersized ones are brought up to size by the addition of a strip of fabric. Cut-down Ann and Andy blocks or parts of them appear in alternate pieced strips. The cut-off pieces from oversized blocks are the basis for further improvisations. □

Eli Leon of Oakland, CA, writes about African-American quiltmaking, including Who'd a Thought It: Improvisation in African-American Quiltmaking *(a show catalog published in 1987 by The San Francisco Craft and Folk Art Museum from which parts of this article have been taken.) Photos of quilts by Sharon Risedorph, except where noted; photos of quilters by the author.*

Angelia Tobias and a friend hold up an "uncompleted" quilt top. (Photo by author)

In her final "restructured" version, Tobias has cut off the bottom third of the quilt and moved the lower part of the cut-off section to the top, dramatically changing the quilt's appearance. She has also restructured within the strips. The same sequence of patches at the left-hand edge of the wide central strip also appears in the large block just right of center in the same strip, rotated 180°. Quilted by Irene Bankhead. (Photo by author)

Leon believes that this 19th-century "Improvisational Strip" quilt (84 in. x 86 in.) is African-American. He seeks help from anyone who might recognize it or be able to direct him to the dealer who sold it in about 1985 at the Ann Arbor Antiques Market. (Photo by Geoffry Johnson)

Quilt Geometry
Getting the angle on puzzle quilts

by Rebecca Speakes with Diane Fitzgerald

a logical crazy quilt? Sounds unlikely, but that's what I make. I guess that's what you get when you take a mathematics student, give her a job as a graphic artist, and teach her quiltmaking. I like a greater challenge than square graph paper and rectangular-shaped quilts offer.

Although I use traditional techniques to put my quilts together, I don't use a traditional block to build them. Instead, I play with geometric puzzle pieces—triangles, trapezoids, parallelograms, and hexagons. I connect lines and points on an angled grid to arrange these angled shapes into a repeat unit that will form the basis of my quilt design. My "block" (detail photo, facing page) is a piece of an interlocking puzzle, the eye dazzler that I aim for.

Designing a quilt

I begin my design at a smaller scale than the finished quilt by drawing a grid on a large piece of vellum, a type of heavy tracing paper. The grid consists of two sets of evenly spaced parallel lines that intersect at an angle. I don't use 60° or 90° angles, because they're more regular and result in equilateral or right triangles—shapes with less action and surprise. I might use 65°, 70°, or 75° as the angle of intersection.

Having drawn her initial grid of parallel lines intersecting at a 65° angle, Rebecca Speakes rotates the grid at a convenient working angle and begins to connect grid lines and points to create the puzzle shapes.

After taping my grid to the drawing board, I put another piece of vellum over it. Using a T square and triangles, I trace over some lines, connecting intersections, while ignoring others to create a puzzle of new interlocking shapes (photo below). The design begins to emerge. To complete it, I put a third layer of vellum over the sketch and trace the final pattern, moving the paper to trace many repeats, all interlocked in the same way, until the paper is covered. If the repeats don't fit together exactly, I add more lines.

Next, I determine the overall, or outer, shape and position the layout within it. Sometimes I rotate it to find the most pleasing arrangement. The outer shape may be a triangle, a rectangle, a square, or other polygon. I also determine the final size at this stage, taking into account the proportion and scale of the pieces in the quilt. This often means that I have to increase the size of the original design.

Scale is an important factor. The pieces must be large enough to be seen clearly and to carry the color and pattern well. My medium-size quilts average 13 to 16 pieces in a single pattern repeat. Although a few of my quilts are miniatures, most are wall quilts. My largest quilt is 98 in. sq. and has 28 pieces per repeat. The smallest pieces are only 1½ in. on a side. Usually there are from 400 to 700 pieces per quilt.

I look at the design both close up and from a distance to see that there is directional movement with an interesting angular line for the eye to follow. Sometimes I like the line to abruptly switch directions, creating a pattern wave. I also look to see what unusual shapes may be created by two or more pieces of different colors. It's important to avoid staccato movement and unpleasing or inconsistent shapes.

To draw the pattern full size, I begin by redrawing a portion of the grid, multiplying the distance between grid lines by the intended increase. For example, lines that I originally drew 1 in. apart I must redraw 4 in. apart if the design is to be increased four times. Then I draw full-scale one entire repeat and part of another below it and

three or four horizontally to make sure that the pattern is drawn correctly and that everything matches up. I number each piece within one repeat. Then I count the total number of repeats. Since the repeats will all be identical, I know how many of each numbered piece will be cut from a particular color or pattern of fabric.

Working out the colors

After completing the geometric design, I think about color. I work almost exclusively with chintz and, although it isn't the easiest fabric to quilt, its crispness and tight weave enable me to use small seams, usually ⅛ in. Limiting the fabric also gives the quilt a consistency of color and texture. Ironically, the hard-finished sheen of the fabric softens the colors, giving each color a connectedness to all the others. I've recently started inserting sparing touches of lamé as highlights. I also occasionally use polished-cotton prints, choosing ones with frequent repeats so I don't have to buy many yards of fabric to get the 30 to 40 identical pieces required. I like graphically strong prints because they hold their own within an already complex pattern.

My fabric supply consists of close to 200 colors of chintz in 1-yd. to 4-yd. lengths. I don't sort them by color but allow their randomness in storage to be part of the inspiration for new color combinations. My favorite colors are blues, greens, and purples, but I've come to appreciate all colors because of the way they blend with, or complement, each other. I keep a record of the colors I have on hand with swatches, as well as those I've used in each quilt. To check color interaction, I carry my swatches along when shopping and am careful to view the fabrics in natural light.

Each quilt has 12 to 18 colors, including at least one color that I've never used. Some-

Speakes' puzzle quilt, "Penny Candy," facing page, top, invites attention. Although it doesn't have a traditional block form, complex geometric shapes form a repeat (detail, right), which steps across the face of the nonstandard shape.

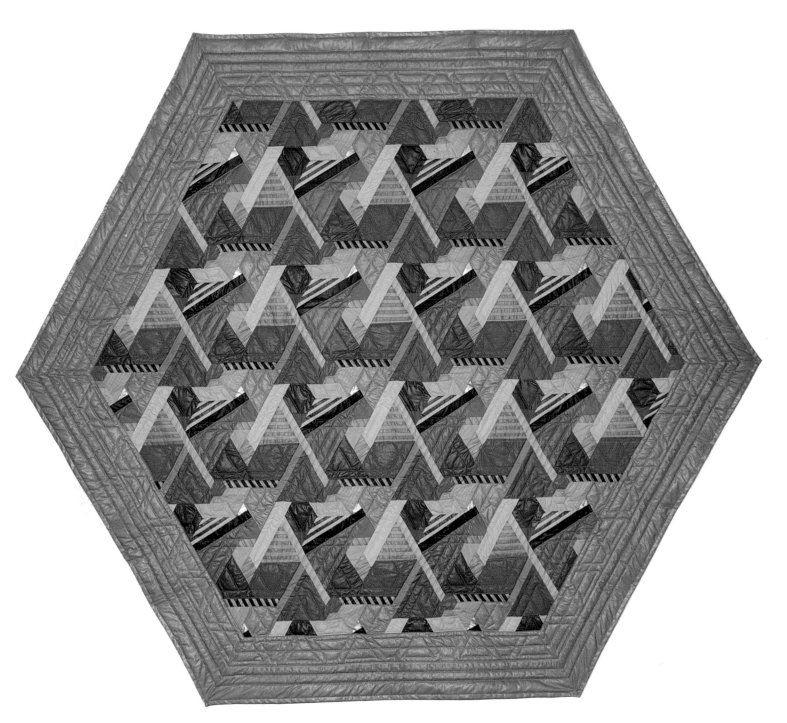

times I start by looking through my supply of fabric. I might lay the pieces out on the floor and sort through them. Sometimes I have an idea of how I want the quilt to look—maybe concentrating on combinations of colors, such as purples and greens or dark or medium palettes. From there, I add many more colors.

Although I don't consciously try to create a mood with a quilt, the colors I select create one. For example, a quilt made up of gold, yellow, cream, peach, lemon chintz, and gold lamé, makes one think of morning sunshine. I like to have tension between the colors, as well as something unexpected, and make sure that each color is distinguishable from its neighbors.

The process of selecting colors for a quilt may take me two or three days. At this point, I don't try to determine the proportion of each color in the quilt, because I don't know where each will be used. It's easy to get the first six or seven colors that work really well together, but the last colors can be difficult to add. I usually start with the blues, greens, reds, and purples and go on to the yellows and oranges. Sometimes yellow never makes it in, or I may use it as a tan or muted yellow.

After selecting the palette, I decide where to use each color, considering the important shapes that bring out the rhythm and action. I give these the eye-catching colors. I generally start with a small shape and use a bright color, like red. I assign the least important colors last. I look for the interplay of darks and lights or for colors that definitely don't work together, such as those that are similar in value. I don't put red and purple together, because both are highlighting colors, and I prefer to distribute them throughout the design, rather than clump them. Often the colors that don't go together may be the determining factor in a layout. At this point, I may drop some colors or add others.

After I've drawn the pattern and determined the outer shape, I decide whether to use stripes during the designing. Stripes emphasize the direction of the pattern, separate pieces that touch, or enliven and add a dynamic quality to a shape that might otherwise be lost. Sometimes I sew strips together to make stripes, and I've also made striped fabric with a permanent marker.

Using colored pencils, I color a section of the scale drawing as a final check to see how it will actually look (photo below). Sometimes I even cut pieces from the fabric and lay them out to see how they'll work together.

Making templates and cutting fabric

To make the templates, I trace the life-size drawing of one repeat of the design on semi-opaque plastic sheets (white translucent matte-finish high-impact styrene, .028 thickness) and cut the shapes apart with scissors. I cut the templates to actual size with no seam allowances and check that they fit together precisely. Then I number each template with the number corresponding to that of the original pattern.

To cut the fabric pieces, I turn the template upside down and trace around it on the back of one layer of fabric. A sharp lead pencil works well on light fabrics, and a red ballpoint pen is good on dark fabrics. I don't like to use light-colored pencils, because they don't stay sharp enough for more than a line or two. I don't worry about cutting a precise seam allowance, because I sew the seams according to the traced lines rather than the edge of the fabric. I ignore the grain lines partly to use the fabric most efficiently but also because the pieces fit together better this way.

Assembling the top

I assemble all the repeats and then join them. It isn't easy to determine which two pieces should go together first. I usually start with two pieces that have one seam in common and sew all these pairs together. I use a sewing machine and backstitch at the beginning and end of each seam. Then I add another piece to these new shapes, and so on. I sew from point to point so that I can later sew odd corners more easily and

precisely. Where four or more points come together, I check the alignment before sewing the final seam.

Assembling the pieces into a top takes about four to six weeks, since I can devote only off-hours to the project, and most tops take well over 80 hours to sew. Because of the complexity of each design, each quilt must be assembled differently.

After I've sewn all the pieces together into a complete top, I iron the top and then place it face down on a sheet on the floor. Looking at the paper pattern for the outer shape, which may be a triangle, a rectangle, or some other polygon, I decide where to mark the top for cutting. The pieced top usually doesn't match the paper pattern exactly. Here and there I may find it necessary to rip out stitches and resew. I may need to fill in a piece or move part of a repeat to another edge.

Starting with a point at a corner and using a T square, a large ruler, and a triangle, I draw the outer edge, making sure that the corners are the proper angle for the shape and that the lines are straight before I cut. Then I trim the excess with scissors. I iron the top again, pressing the seams in the direction that works best. Lamé should be ironed on the wrong side, as direct heat may remove the color coating.

I add the border next. Including the binding, the border contains at least three colors and usually four or five. I often determine these colors by the amount of fabric that's left, as I usually use colors from the quilt for the border. I use chintz for the border, as well as for the back and binding.

I cut the binding at the same time as the border, using the "tube" method for cutting a continuous bias strip (drawing, facing page). The binding may be the same color as the outer border of the quilt or a

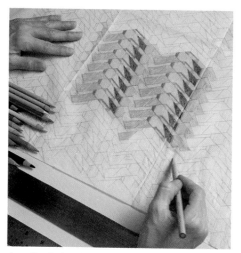

As a final check on her fabric color selections, Speakes uses colored pencils to shade in eight vertical and two horizontal repeats of the design on the scale drawing.

contrasting color. To calculate the square inches of fabric that I'll need for the binding, I measure the perimeter of the quilt and multiply this number by the total width of the binding (I usually use doubled binding for my quilts, cutting it 1¾ in. wide). I add 20% for miters and waste. Then I divide by the width of the binding fabric to get the length of fabric needed.

After sewing the border to the top with mitered corners, I assemble the top, batting, and backing and pin the layers together with straight pins. Then I trim the excess batting and backing to match the top, and I baste the three layers together with stitches winding back and forth, primarily through the areas to be quilted (bottom photo, facing page). After I've thoroughly basted the quilt, I machine-stitch the two raw edges of the folded chintz bias binding to the right side of the top, fold it to the back, and hand-stitch the folded edge in place with an invisible hemstitch.

Quilting and finishing

The quilting pattern often echoes the angles and design of the puzzle pattern, and I repeat a portion of the design in the border quilting. Rather than mark the quilt, I use transparent tape as a guide for quilting lines, which run about ⅛ in. parallel to the seamlines; I seldom quilt in the ditch. I quilt on my lap without a frame or hoop. Chintz is a little tough to quilt, and I've bent a few of the size 8 betweens from S. Thomas and Sons (Redditch, England) on it. I don't quilt the highlighting pieces or the lamé, because I want them to stand out.

The final touch is to embroider my initials, RMS, and the year in thin block letters on the back of each quilt. A *c* in a circle indicates that the design is copyrighted.

To date, I've started 43 quilts and completed 33. I like to experiment with pattern and see my designs becoming more complex, more removed from the grid on which they're based. If you want to develop your ability, you have to make it one of your highest priorities and really devote yourself to it. For me, this means using all my energy on one medium and exploring it to the fullest. □

Rebecca Speakes usually exhibits two or three quilts a year in the Minnesota Quilters' annual show and with David Omer Interior Design Associates of Minneapolis, MN. One of her latest, "Heat Wave," was selected for Quilt National's International Tour for the next 2½ years. Diane Fitzgerald is a member of Surface Design Minnesota, Minnesota Quilters, and is pursuing a degree in design at the University of Minnesota in Minneapolis. All photos by Jerry Robb.

Cutting a continuous bias strip

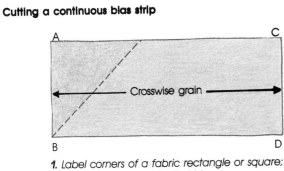

1. Label corners of a fabric rectangle or square; fold down corner A to find bias.

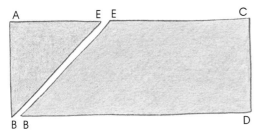

2. Mark bias fold line.
Cut off triangle formed on fold line.

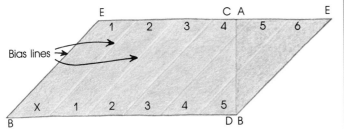

Bias lines

3. Sew triangle to end C-D with ¼-in. seamline. Sew seam twice to lock stitches.

4. Determine desired width of bias binding: measure cording or seam being covered, add a little for turning, add ½ in. for two ¼-in. seams. Mark cutting lines parallel to bias line across fabric, and number strips as shown.

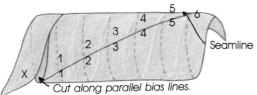

Seamline

Cut along parallel bias lines.

5. Pin crosswise edges, right sides together, matching numbered sections. X stands alone. Sew with a ¼-in. seam twice. Shake tube out.

6. Cut a continuous strip along drawn line, starting at X and cutting through seams.

Instructions adapted from method given in *Coats & Clark's Sewing Book: Newest Methods A to Z* (Western Publishing Co. 1976)

Suggested bias widths:

Piping with ¼-in. cording—1½-in. binding

Plain binding for ¼-in. seams—1¼-in. binding

Doubled binding for extra thickness—2-in. binding, 1¾ in. for quilt

Illustration by Lainé Roundy

After she has completed the top and marked the outline of the border on the wrong side, Speakes carefully trims away the excess, then sews on an assembled border. Below, she pins the three layers of the quilt together with straight pins and bastes in a winding pattern, sewing mostly in areas to be quilted.

By varying the colors and the lengths of the log strips, Larzelere creates nontraditional versions of the Log Cabin quilt pattern. "Black/Plum/Teal," 100% cotton, 82 in. x 72 in., ©1984 Judith Larzelere.

Log Cabins
A traditional quilt pattern with a 20th-century look

by Judith Ann Larzelere

One of the most popular quilt designs that were developed in the 19th century was the Log Cabin. A small square, often red in traditional quilts, at the center of each block denotes the hearth—the center of the pioneer home. Rectangular pieces laid end to end around this square represent the logs of the settler's cabin. By alternating light and dark strips of fabric, quilters composed blocks that used value and color for design interest. I'd like to explain traditional Log Cabin construction and show how I alter and adapt the techniques to create nontraditional designs.

Traditional designs

In the two main variations of the Log Cabin block—the Log Cabin and the Courthouse Steps—each block starts from the small center square, but the surrounding "logs" are sewn in different order. Log Cabin strips are sewn around the center square, with the length of each new strip matching the side of the existing block; Courthouse Steps strips are sewn alternately on opposite sides of the square.

The design interest of a Log Cabin depended on a diagonal through the center of the block, which divided it into areas of light and dark values. Hundreds of fabric scraps were used in almost any order to emphasize value change, as shown in the drawings below.

Several patterns for "setting," or arranging, the blocks into the quilt top evolved as the individual blocks were turned to make use of their diagonal divisions of value. Three popular traditional Log Cabin quilt

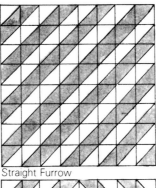
Straight Furrow

Barn Raising

Streak O'Lightning

variations are illustrated above. Over 1,000 possible designs have been calculated by computer.

Changing the traditions

Let's look at some ways to alter the traditional Log Cabin designs without moving away from the rectangular, overlapped logs. It's possible to simply vary the width of the strips, change the block shape, move the center square, and arrange color values other than diagonally—or combine any of these steps.

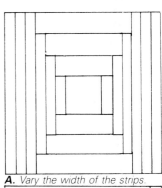
A. Vary the width of the strips.

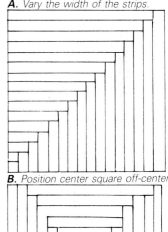
B. Position center square off-center.

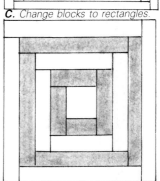
C. Change blocks to rectangles.

D. Alternate colors and/or values.

Striped and two-tone strips— These strips can produce simple, yet startling, variations. The process for making them is derived from Seminole piecing. Strips of colors are cut and resewn to create a pieced band, which is then

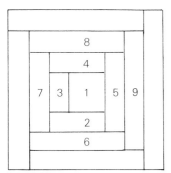

			8			
			4			
7	3	1		5	9	
			2			
			6			

Log Cabin

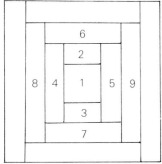

		6		
		2		
8	4	1	5	9
		3		
		7		

Courthouse Steps

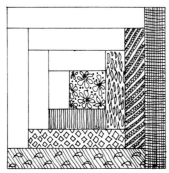

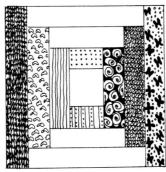

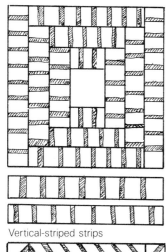

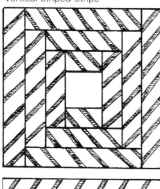

Vertical-striped strips

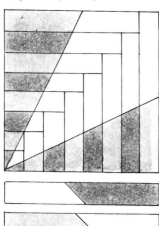

Diagonal-striped strips

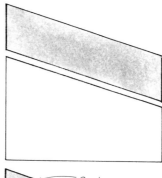

Two-tone strips

cut through the stripes perpendicularly or at an angle; the strips are restitched in a new arrangement.

To make these strips, cut fabric into 1½-in. to 4-in. widths. The number you cut depends on how often the background will be interrupted by contrasting stripes. Make them as long as the fabric is wide. Count the number of sections and cut that many ¾-in. or wider strips of a contrasting color. Alternating the background and contrasting-color strips, join all pieces with ¼-in. seams until a new pieced cloth is

formed. Press all the seams open. You can cut across the cloth for vertical-striped strips, or on a diagonal for diagonal-striped strips.

To make two-tone strips, cut two contrasting cloths on a diagonal, and seam them together to form a rectangle. With a marker, rule off strips, including a ¼-in. seam allowance on each side, and cut along the guidelines. To use the two-tone strips in an effective design, mark the muslin sewing guide with the

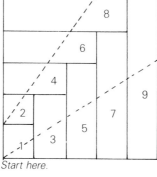

Cut here.

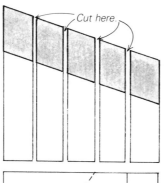

Start here.

diagonal placement lines as well as the stitching lines. Construction proceeds from the starting square outward on alternate sides.

Large-block quilts—Traditionally, Log Cabin blocks ranged from 6 in. sq. to about 12 in. sq. The design depended on patterns that were created with dozens of these squares. However, if there are fewer blocks, and if the size of each block is increased, say to a 36-in. square or 30-in. by 40-in. rectangle, some interesting symmetrical shapes are possible.

Four large blocks can be set together to form a quilt. They are made separately by the third method of Log Cabin construction, illustrated on page 48. The Nested-Square pattern is the hardest to complete, as the logs' short edges must be joined in the central seams for a matched pattern and an even look.

By closely watching the value and intensity of the colors, you can produce an advancing or a receding rectangle of nearly any size from one large block, as shown

Cross

Star

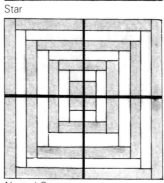

Nested Squares

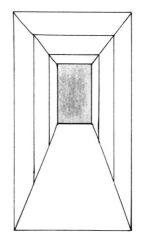

in the drawing below at left. If the darkest color in the quilt is placed in the center, the center recedes; if the lightest color is placed there, the center advances. This design works especially well with striped strips. Before purchasing fabric, you should make several color studies.

Another variation on a large-block quilt is the pyramid image shown above. The basic idea comes from Courthouse Steps. To emphasize its shape, the pyramid is a fabric of a contrasting value from the other three quadrants. Two large pyramid blocks can be set together to form a jar, pot, or lantern shape. Variety comes from experimenting with proportions and moving away from exact symmetry.

All the designs I've discussed thus far are based on an even number of strips applied around a central starting point. If the strips are not applied evenly, some design possibiities open up. The strips must always cover the raw edges of those already stitched down, but there does not have to be regularity of placement.

The quilt shown at right is made up of two Courthouse Steps blocks. "Blue Jar," 72 in. x 48 in., 100% cotton, ©1984 Judith Larzelere.

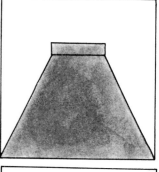

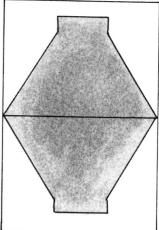

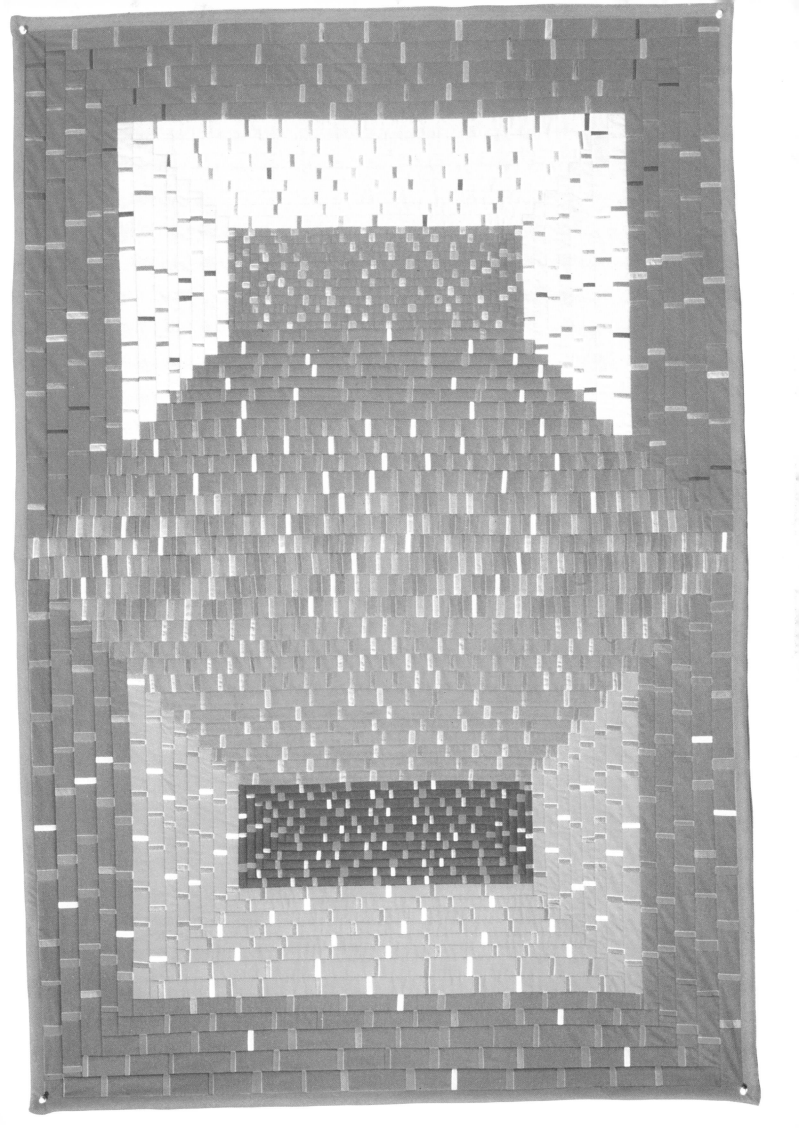

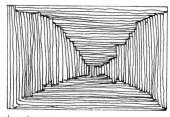

Landscape

Traditional construction

There are two methods for piecing the traditional blocks. In the first method, each block is pieced by hand or machine. The time spent in measuring and cutting all the log strips is considerable, however, and piecing must be very exact. To keep the block square, you can mark the ¼-in. seam allowances or check the work periodically with a right-angle gauge. The blocks are then assembled into a quilt top, which is basted to batting and backing, hand-quilted or tied off, and finished with binding. Tying off is done with a cotton cord or yarn that is drawn through all the layers of the assembled quilt. Knots, placed at regular intervals on the back of the quilt, hold the layers together and prevent the batting from bunching. In traditional quilts, very often the knots were placed on the front as an additional decorative element.

In the second method of construction, all the stitching guidelines for the block are drawn onto a square of muslin. The center square of fabric is pinned in place on the muslin pattern, right side up. Strips of a selected width, commonly ½ in., are cut from lengths of fabric. They don't need to be premeasured for length, because that is easily determined by the muslin pattern when they are sewn. One at a time, the strips are placed right side down along the seam guidelines on top of the center square, cut to length with ¼-in. seam allowances, and then pinned and stitched down. The strip is turned to open away from the center and pressed flat. A second strip is then laid right side down along the seam guideline of the square and the short end of the previous strip, as shown in the drawing below. The rest of the strips are applied in the same way: Each newly sewn strip is lapped over the raw edges of the strips sewn down before, and the work progresses from the small center square outward to the edges. All the outer edges end up free on top of the pattern. The advantages of this method are the speed and accuracy of stitching, made possible by the muslin pattern.

After all the blocks are constructed, they are assembled into the quilt top. Each block is seamed to the next through the outer edge of the outermost strip and the muslin pattern; this way, the finished quilt top is already lined with muslin. Sometimes the quilt is simply backed and tied with no batting added (very common in velvet quilts), then bound.

A third method

I use a construction technique that eliminates the finishing processes of quilting or tying off the top, batting, and backing. A muslin stitching guide is prepared for each block, then basted to squares of batting and backing, as when a miniature quilt is made. The block is pressed to reduce the loft of the batting. The center square of fabric is pinned over the muslin guide, and the light and dark strips are laid down one at a time. The strips are pinned, sewn, and pressed open just as in the second method described above—but with a difference. This time, the strips are stitched together through all three layers of the prepared block, so the block is pieced and quilted in the same step. The outermost strips are still kept free of the muslin at the block edges. All the stitching threads are pulled up from the bottom and tied off as each strip is sewn down.

The blocks are sewn together to form the quilt top in two steps: First, the individual blocks are sewn together in rows the length or width of the quilt; then, the rows are joined together until the entire quilt is assembled. To join the blocks, place two of them right sides together. Pin, mark, and sew together the outer edges of two strips, one from each block, while keeping all the other parts (muslin, batting, backing) free. Next, open the blocks and trim the batting and backing as necessary so the backs of the two joining blocks overlap smoothly and conceal the seam of the front pieces. Hem the backing from one block onto the backing of the other by hand, with seam allowances turned under, to close the block. Continue joining blocks together to form rows; then join the rows together in the same way.

Finishing

A binding finishes all the remaining raw edges. To make a binding, cut strips across the grain. For a quilt with a 1-in. border, cut strips 2½ in. wide and join enough lengths together to go around the perimeter of the quilt. (For a 72-in. by 36-in. quilt, you would need 218 in. of binding: 72 in. + 72 in. + 36 in. + 36 in. + two ¼-in. seam allowances for each strip). Join the strips with diagonal seams to make a continuous binding; sew the binding onto the right side of the quilt along the quilt's outer seam line. After you've trimmed all the edges of the batting to 1 in., hem the binding by hand to the back of the quilt. To hang the quilt on the wall, sew a 3-in. to 4-in. sleeve to the top back of the quilt, and stitch it, leaving the ends open so that you can insert a pole.

I have been experimenting with Log Cabin construction for a year and a half. I hope this summary of my discoveries will inspire you to explore the rich possibilities of the Log Cabin design in your own quilt making. □

Judith Ann Larzelere is an artist in Newbury, MA. Her quilts were selected for Quilt National '81, '83, and '85. She lectures and conducts workshops on color and Log Cabin variations. Photos by author.

Log Cabin construction

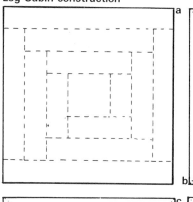
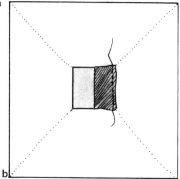
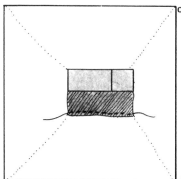
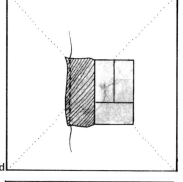

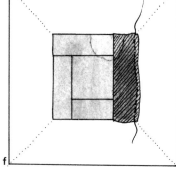

Pillows by Jane Goo, clockwise from top: Cactus, Buttercup, Anthurium, Plumeria.

to her exquisite quilting is to quilt one row's width out from the design each time so the connections where the lines from each section join will be smooth.

After the center third of the inner medallion is completed, the quilting is continued out to the edges on both sides. Then the quilt is rolled on the frame and quilted section by section until one end is reached. Next it is rolled in the opposite direction so the other half can be quilted.

Jane Vegas suggests a thumb thimble rather than one that's used on the middle finger. It allows quilting in any direction, which is helpful if one side of the frame is inaccessible. A thumb thimble can also eliminate some of the frequent turning a hoop frame requires. Sizes 7 and 8 needles are commonly used for quilting. Jane Goo recommends sewing the finish binding on by hand, as a machine-stitched binding will be tighter and will pull the quilt out of shape when it is washed. Additional tips from experts include cutting the backing piece slightly larger than the top to allow for take-up in the quilting process and, to make the quilting easier, piecing the three layers of fabric so that the seams on the top and back do not overlap.

Akana advises: "When you are making [a quilt] for someone else, you are sharing part of yourself. It's important to share the best part, so make the quilt for someone else, and the work will flow beautifully." □

Sue Ellen White-Hansen is a free-lance photo-journalist and consultant based on Whidbey Island, WA. She'd like to say mahalo to the quilters of Hawaii. Photos by author, except where noted.

Further reading

Akana, Elizabeth A. *Hawaiian Quilting: A Fine Art,* 1981. Available from Kauai Museum, Box 248, Lihue, HI 96766. *History, analysis, technique, photos.*

Inns, Helen. *Your Hawaiian Quilt: How to Make It,* 1957. Available from Kauai Museum, Box 248, Lihue, HI 96766. *Shows how to make a full-size quilt with many photos and drawings.*

Jones, Stella M. *Hawaiian Quilts,* 2nd ed. Honolulu: Daughters of Hawaii, Honolulu Academy of Arts and Mission Houses Museum, 1974. *History, legends, technique.*

Plews, Edith Rice. *Hawaiian Quilting on Kauai.* Lihue, HI: Kauai Museum, 1976. *Keynote address, photos from largest exhibition of Hawaiian quilts (1933).*

Stevens, Napua. *The Hawaiian Quilt.* Honolulu: Service Printers, 1971. *Good how-to book for small pieces.*

Titcomb, Margaret. *The Ancient Hawaiians: How They Clothed Themselves.* (Hawaii's Cultural Heritage Series, Vol. 1). Honolulu: Hogarth Press, 1974. *On clothing arts, tools, work patterns.*

blends tend to pop out. Others have found that polyester blends are easier for students to handle and are more durable.

Appliqué and assembly—The appliquéing of the design layer is begun at the center of the pattern and worked outward in progressively wider sections. The most common technique is to turn under ⅛ in. to ¼ in. with a small needle for 1 in. along an edge and overcast with small stitches. Jane Goo finds that a narrower hem turns out, requiring deeper and more visible overcasting. The thread for the appliqué normally matches the color of the design layer.

When the top is completed, which, for a full-size quilt, takes Goo about six months of part-time work, it is laid on the batting and a fabric backing. Some quilters baste the layers together. Others roll them on the quilting frame and stitch. The frame stretches and holds the layers taut. When a smaller hoop frame is used, basting is required.

Polyester is the most common batting material, but Goo prefers Japanese cotton. "It should be about one-half inch thick and is the best for quilting," she says, "because the quilt will puff up in the sun." It comes in rolls of four layers; Goo uses three of them for her batts. Although harder to quilt than the two polyester layers she alternately uses, and more costly—about $30 per roll (a full-size quilt requires four rolls)—Goo feels that the cotton is worth it, given the time it takes to complete a quilt. The cotton batting available on the U.S. mainland will not work, so mainland quilters should use polyester or wool.

Quilting—Quilting in the Hawaiian manner is a benchmark of the art in style and technique. Graceful parallel quilting lines follow the appliquéd design and flow to the edge in undulating waves. Where spaces narrow, the quilting lines come together and end.

The Hawaiian quilting frame (right photo, page 51) is constructed of sawhorses and 2x4s. Wooden dowels or metal pins allow adjustments for mounting. The quilting is worked in sections, the middle third of the mounted quilt first. Beginning at the *piko,* the stitches outline the center design and are followed by successive parallel quilting lines. Most experts keep the quilting lines ½ in. to ¾ in. apart so the finished piece stays soft and pliable and the stitching is accentuated. Deborah Kepola Kakalia, a well-known quilter and teacher, says the trick

Designing Oriental Quilts

Traditional patchwork and appliqué inspired by Persian carpets

by Judy P. Cloninger

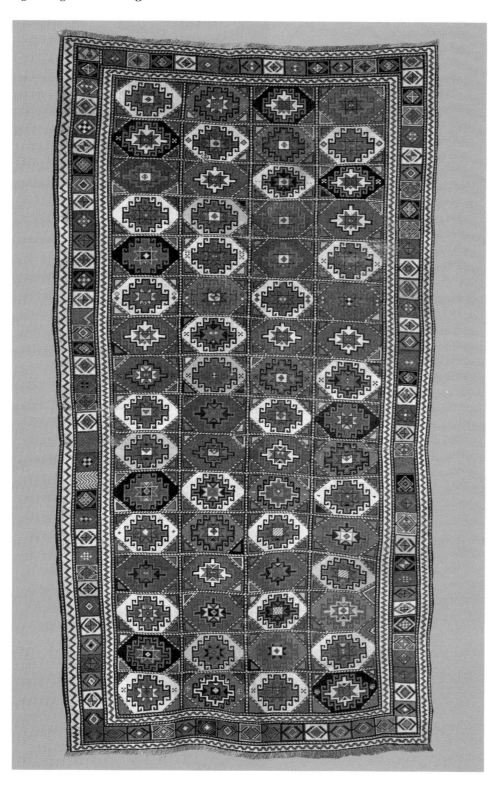

*a*lthough the path from Oriental rug to quilt offers surprising twists and turns, the ground isn't all that unfamiliar. A look at Oriental rugs through the quilter's eye reveals lots of exciting similarities. Many rugs feature geometric shapes familiar to quilters, such as the nine-patch and eight-pointed stars, and a field is often composed of blocks framed by borders.

The images seem strange, yet familiar, for two reasons. First, American quilters have assimilated designs from popular 19th-century Eastern fabrics and carpets. Second, the format of quilts and rugs is intrinsically similar, which has led to the development of parallel design structures.

Both weavers and quilters manipulate colors and shapes to form designs on a flexible, flat surface, and Oriental rugs can inspire contemporary quiltmakers. Since the textile techniques are very different, though, it's a challenge to achieve the effect of a rug in quilting, and I'm developing a new form of quilt design from the best of both worlds.

Field designs in rugs and quilts—Both rugs and quilts present major motifs in a central field or ground surrounded by borders. Most field designs on rugs and quilts can be placed in one of three categories: central medallion, blocks, or repeated motifs.

The *central-medallion* field is composed of a large geometric or floral motif that's placed in the center, surrounded by secondary motifs, and enclosed by multiple borders of varying widths. Many 18th- and 19th-century American quilts, such as the "Bethlehem Star," feature a central medallion, like the jewel-medallion Oriental rugs.⇨

In her 69-in. x 96-in. quilt, "Shiraz" (right), Judy Cloninger combined Oriental-style fabrics in a conventional patchwork manner to produce a block quilt. But to lighten the blocks and create a lacier look around their edges, as in the ornate Shirvan rug at left, she greatly increased the number of pieces. (Photo at right by John Hunt; photo at left courtesy of the Metropolitan Museum of Art, New York City)

From *Threads* magazine (June 1988) 17:46-51

The elegant 16th-century silk Kashan rug (p. 58), shows the highest development of the medallion concept. The floral star at the center provides inspiration for the rich floral field and elaborate multiple borders. While I haven't made a central-medallion rug quilt, flowers like these provided inspiration for my "Caliph's Puzzle" quilt.

In *block designs,* the second major category of field structures, the field is divided into sections called blocks, and the design motif is repeated in each block. The blocks are enclosed by horizontal and vertical bands called sashing, or lattice, by quilters. Sometimes the sashing is diagonal, and the blocks are set on their points. Often the artisan varies the colors or subtly changes the design from one block to the next to produce interesting modifications.

Block designs are frequently found in Oriental rugs. In the Shirvan rug from the Caucasus (p. 54), the rectangular blocks are divided by a narrow sashing. Each octagonal *gul* (the word means *flower* and is applied to an octagonal motif employed by the Turkoman tribes) is composed of a stepped polygon with projecting hooks. The star in the center of each *gul* resembles the American patchwork pattern "Ohio Star."

My block-design quilt, "Shiraz" (p. 55), is based on geometric designs produced in the villages near the Persian city of Shiraz. This block design probably derived from the eight-pointed star, which has evolved in many interesting variations.

The third major field-design structure is an *overall pattern created by a small, repeated unit.* In quilts, this is often a simple geometric shape. Patterns well-known to quilters are the hexagonal "Grandmother's Flower Garden," the triangular "Thousand Pyramids," the square "Boston Common," and the 60° diamond "Baby Blocks."

Eastern artisans are also fond of the repeated unit. To them, it suggests eternity, a pattern with no beginning or end. Such patterns are often found in Islamic floor and wall tiles and in intricate rugs. The single repeated unit also appears in many carpets in the shape of the paisley or *boteh* (stylized leaf) motif, often set in staggered rows to form a diagonal pattern.

"Caliph's Puzzle" (facing page) is an example of the repeated-design unit. I started with the eight-pointed star but substituted squares for opposite pairs of diamonds to make a six-pointed elongated star. These alternate horizontally and vertically on the

field of geometric shapes (diamonds, squares, trapezoids, and right triangles) arranged like a puzzle mosaic. The drawing on the facing page shows how the pieces fit together. The design is simple, as far as the number of pieces goes, but it looks complicated.

The three types of field designs may be viewed as a progression from large to small. The *central medallion* can be simplified and reduced in size, and it can appear as *blocks* repeated in rows on the field. Further reduction and simplification can occur, until a *single motif* is arranged in even more numerous rows on the field.

Designing with Oriental fabrics—Fabric is crucial in my Oriental quilts. I use paisleys, small geometrics, exotic floral and leaf patterns, and running vines—any pattern that evokes the Oriental theme. Some of the fabrics in the source list on the facing page are expensive, but considering the cost of the labor that goes into a quilt, no matter how much you spend on fabric, it will be only a small percentage of the quilt's value. To get just the right print or motif, I've spent up to $100/yd., but usually I can find the colors and patterns I need for much less. Sometimes I also overdye yardage, par-

Cloninger gives a lot of time and thought to each block she creates. She experiments with many colors, prints, and borders before she is satisfied. Neutral background fabric forms the basis of this eight-pointed star, and depth is produced by the interplay of dark triangles and light and dark borders.

ticularly neutrals, to change the shade slightly or to add patina for a richer effect.

Many designs in printed fabrics today derive from India cottons introduced to Europe by the Dutch and British East India traders in the 17th century. Even further back, textile designs in India were influenced by Oriental carpet design. Field structures and individual motifs became part of the design lexicon of India. Lotuses, carnations, tulips, and roses became favorite floral motifs. Chintzes, calicos, and paisleys are all Indian designs with Oriental roots.

My earlier Oriental quilts are pieced entirely of such fabrics. I try out color ranges and fabrics with different patterns and intensities, as shown in the photo on the facing page. I combine neutral background prints, solids, and larger prints. Then I add different border prints and widths. If I start with a light, bright star, I'll use mostly dark, rich colors and patterns lightened with bright border prints to make the star seem to rise slightly from the plane of the fabric. A dark star will tend to recede. Borders are crucial in controlling the interplay of light and dark and in adding depth.

In "Caliph's Puzzle," I used an appliqué technique rather than piecing to create a blend of contemporary cottons printed with Oriental motifs. The rich colors and intricate patterns of "Caliph's Puzzle" suggest the opulence and resources available to that wealthy class of Eastern rulers.

The quilt is based on a 17th-century rug woven in India, which was a composite of Persian, Egyptian, and Indian designs. I embellished the field by cutting apart printed florals and paisleys and reassembling them in a miniature *broderie perse* fashion to create entirely new flowers and designs. And the whole border is constructed in *broderie perse* (see "Composing an Oriental flower in *broderie perse*," p. 59) to create fanciful flowers and vines.

One of my objectives in "Caliph's Puzzle" was to blend many diverse printed cottons to produce a new and homogeneous fabric—to achieve the tapestry effect of an elaborate Oriental rug throughout the field and orders. Another of my objectives was to imitate the fanciful, imaginative palmettes of Oriental rugs, like the Kashan rug on p. 58, with my stylized flowers and vines. ⇨

Intrigued by the geometry of the translation from rug to quilt, Cloninger finds the mosaic field inspiring. In "Caliph's Puzzle" (35 in. x 52 in.), a field of simple geometric shapes that construct a repeated unit fit together in a complex mosaic pattern. (Photo by David Lund)

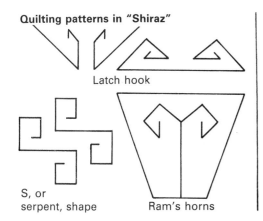

Quilting patterns in "Shiraz"

Latch hook

S, or serpent, shape

Ram's horns

Repeated motif (composed of diamonds and squares)

Diamond

Trapezoid

Square

Right triangle

Small square

In "Caliph's Puzzle," a few simple geometric shapes are fitted together into an intricate pattern.

This 16th-century Kashan rug has a central medallion featuring palmettes. (Photo courtesy of The Metropolitan Museum of Art, New York City)

Designing with Oriental motifs—The center of each octagonal block on the rug that inspired "Shiraz" had probably begun as an eight-pointed star, one of the most popular Oriental motifs; but four of the points had been deleted. I used squared triangles for the two horizontal pairs of points (photo, p. 55). I brought light into my stars by using bright and dark colors for alternating rays, and I enhanced the block's elongated appearance by placing a pair of mitered rectangles around a narrow central rectangle. I divided the blocks into fourths with strips along the horizontal and vertical axes.

To increase the elongated appearance of the field, typical in Oriental rugs, I made the horizontal strips that divide the blocks wider than the vertical ones. I used one other asymmetrical feature on "Shiraz's" field—a diamond at the top and a square at the bottom of each block. After I was satisfied with the Oriental complications I had added, I counted the number of pieces in each block. I discovered that my simple patchwork block had grown from 40 to 144 pieces, which I considered a gross amount. But that's what it took to achieve the Oriental effect I wanted.

The first border is based on barber-pole stripe, a popular Oriental rug border. Two similar borders on each side of the main border, a traditional running vine, reflect another characteristic of many outstanding Oriental rugs—subtle asymmetry in a mostly symmetrical design.

To get more light and depth in the main border, I added float pieces to separate the diagonally set squares from the triangles beneath them. I used a similar technique in "Caliph's Puzzle," outlining each figure of the field with ⅛-in. strips of light-colored fabric to produce a mosaic effect.

I quilted "Shiraz" with Oriental motifs. I used S, or serpent, shapes, latch hooks, and ram's horns, detailed in the lower-left drawing on p. 57.

Accepting the challenge—I began basing my quilt designs on Oriental-rug themes when I recognized the inherent similarities of the two textile arts. Both are designed to produce warmth and beauty for dwellings, either for the bed or floor, and they're the same size—a typical rug is 7 ft. x 9 ft., and a double-size quilt is 84 in. x 108 in. The construction of rugs and quilts is similar in terms of time and labor-intensive handwork on simple wooden frames. In addition, many fine rugs and quilts have been prized and collected through the centuries.

In translating Oriental design concepts into quilts, invention and ingenuity are requisite. The different techniques used by weavers and quilters make exact duplica-tion impossible, so new and creative solutions are necessary. Nevertheless, one can learn a lot from studying Oriental rugs, with an eye toward quilting.

Rugs have taught me how to blend colors and use neutrals to bring light and richness into my work. I've also learned more about geometry from seeing how basic shapes can be changed. If you cut the corners of an eight-pointed star, you get a square; further cutting produces an octagon. I used this concept to design the field of "Caliph's Puzzle." Reciprocal borders like those on "Shiraz" are typical of rugs but not quilts. (Yin and Yang designs, composed of identical meshed shapes, are another example.) Borders, blocks, and flowers often begin as simple shapes that are elaborated into more complex designs, like the palmettes in "Caliph's Puzzle."

In the final analysis, Oriental rugs and American quilts share many common elements, and blending them offers opportunities to create masterworks of design. □

Judy P. Cloninger is an award-winning quiltmaker and a designer, lecturer, and teacher. For the past six years, she has translated Oriental designs into quilts. Her work has appeared in Great American Quilts 1987, Hands All Around: Quilts from Many Nations, *and* Quilt Digest 3.

Composing an Oriental flower in broderie perse

You can create your own fanciful Oriental flowers from an assortment of Oriental motifs, using the technique of *broderie perse* (Persian embroidery). In *broderie perse*, the quilter cuts motifs from printed fabrics, especially 18th-century Oriental florals, and appliqués them with tiny stitches to a background fabric.

The fabric—Collect a wide assortment of fabrics with Oriental motifs in as many shades as possible of your chosen color range. Select paisleys, exotic flowers, small geometrics, and allover prints. Make sure the sizes of the motifs vary.

A fabric that is too dark or intense on the right side might be perfect if you use the wrong side (center swatch, top row, photo at right, below). Neutrals often look richer rinsed in a tan-dye solution (or a more intense shade in the same color family). Experiment with your fabrics and think about ways to improve them.

Flower design—A favorite technique of Eastern rugmakers is to show the flower form in cross section, called a palmette. The flowers appear to be cut in half laterally (drawings below). Thousands of such examples exist. Choose some of your favorites. Rather than try to duplicate in appliqué the palmettes that you see on Oriental rugs, use them to inspire your own appliquéd palmettes. Base your design on the idea of the heart, or center, of a flower surrounded by petals. Next, sketch the border into which the palmette will fit to scale. This will help you determine the scale and proportion of the individual flower (drawing at lower left).

From different fabrics, cut out the palmette parts: petals (paisleys and lozenges), a flower for the heart, and a frame or enclosure for the heart (leaves or vines), as shown in the drawing at lower right. Move the pieces around to try various arrangements,

and assemble this "puzzle" in the way you find most pleasing.

Be imaginative! Your flower doesn't have to be realistic. One reason for the appeal and longevity of this design is its fantasy. The absence of rigid rules allows for great freedom to express your own idea of beauty.

Appliqué—Cut out the pieces that you've selected for your final design with seam allowances. Turn the edges under and appliqué them to neutral background fabric with tiny, hidden stitches (see the article on pp. 65-69), like the palmette in the drawing below.

Repeat this process as many times as you wish to compose different flowers, vines, and other fanciful shapes, as I did in the border and field of "Caliph's Puzzle." One design inspiration can lead to many different flowers if you use various fabrics and arrange the basic pieces differently. —J.P.C.

Cloninger cut out small flowers, paisleys, leaves, sections of borders, etc., and recombined them to create the fanciful flowers and gracefully curved border of "Caliph's Puzzle" (p. 57). (Photo by Harry Gates)

The many different fabrics in "Caliph's Puzzle" were chosen from harmonious shades ranging from cherry to rose and peach to rust, as well as shades of green.

Creating a flower

Some palmettes are representational; others are quite fantastic.

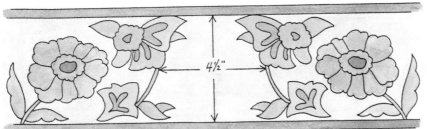

4½"

The palmette must fit the space determined both by the width of the border and its relation to the flowers and vines surrounding it.

Cut flower parts from different fabrics.

Petals

Center enclosure

Center, or heart

Turn under seam allowances and appliqué flower pieces to neutral background.

Illustrations by Laîné Roundy

Clothes for Quilters

Piecing and appliqué transform simple shapes

by Ann Williamson Hyman

i grew up in a home where no one sewed. When a button fell off a blouse or a jacket, putting it back on was a major event. One Christmas, when I was about 13 years old, I asked my mother for a cape. Instead of buying me a cape, she gave me some fabric, a pattern, and an inexpensive sewing machine. I happily cut out the fabric and sewed the pieces together. No one around me knew enough to tell me to rip out my mistakes and redo them, and I bypassed the frustration and tedium that most people experience when they're learning how to sew. I was free to create and experiment.

Perhaps as a result of having had little formal training in sewing, I look upon sewing techniques as a means to implement design rather than as ends in themselves. In my work, I concentrate on creating texture and patterns on simple garment shapes with piecing and appliqué. Every bit of fabric has an inherent geometry, color, and weight that provide an opportunity for expression. I can spend hours walking down the aisles of fabric stores, exploring the bolts of fabric.

Design and fabric—Rectangular-shaped garments are the easiest ones to work with. A Chanel-style jacket, such as the one in the photo at right, and a basic coat, like the one on p. 62, both without any darts, are my mainstays. I vary them with different front closures, with single or double-breasted openings, and with V necks or mandarin collars, but the basic shapes are the same.

First I draw my designs on paper in black and white. I make a lot of these rough

A central panel with bright squares of appliqué creates a high contrast against a dark grid in this simple Chanel-style silk jacket designed and made by Ann Williamson Hyman. (Photo by Anthony Rush Ledbetter)

Coat pattern

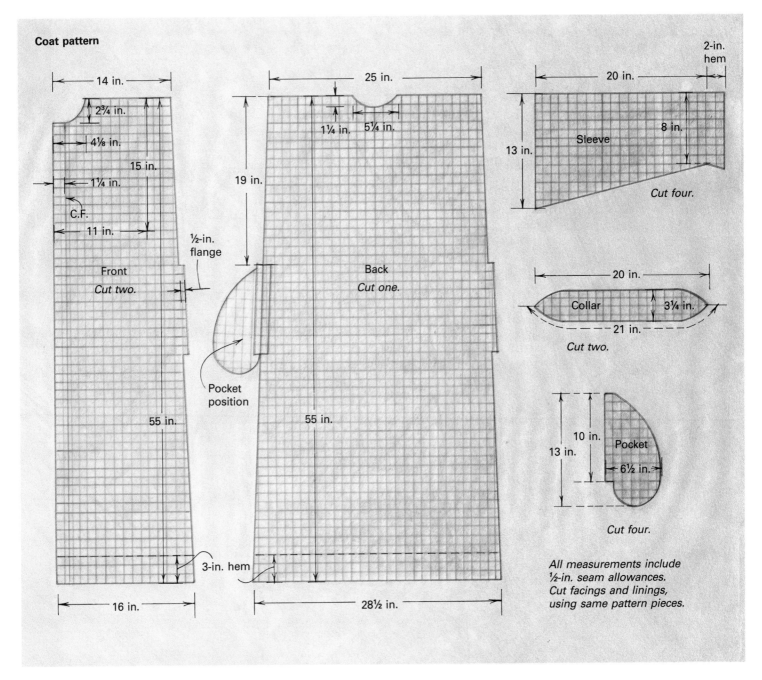

Front
Cut two.

14 in.
2¾ in.
4⅛ in.
15 in.
1¼ in.
C.F.
11 in.
½-in. flange
55 in.
3-in. hem
16 in.

Back
Cut one.

25 in.
1¼ in.
5¼ in.
19 in.
Pocket position
55 in.
28½ in.

Sleeve
Cut four.

2-in. hem
20 in.
8 in.
13 in.

Collar
Cut two.

20 in.
3¼ in.
21 in.

Pocket
Cut four.

13 in.
10 in.
6½ in.

All measurements include ½-in. seam allowances. Cut facings and linings, using same pattern pieces.

---

sketches, from which I choose the ones that work best. Many of my pieces have an architectural quality, in that I break up the surface into "use areas." In my sketches I divide the garment into areas for the shoulder; center, or body; sleeves; and closures. I then work out designs and decorations to highlight these sections. In my "Lightning Coat" (right photo, page 62), for example, one can trace the movement and transformation of the lightning bolts as they pass through the gray and black fields of color. I try to emphasize how the different parts interact and influence each other. When the parts look good, I stand back to make sure the composition works as a whole. Most of my imagery is geometric, with lots of squares, lines, and occasionally triangles. During the sketching period, a mistake, a slip of the pencil, or an exasperated scribble often leads to a new idea.

After I've worked out a satisfactory design, I begin selecting my fabrics. The qual-

ities of color are very complex, so I prefer to work with actual fabrics. In the Pacific Northwest, where I grew up, the sky is often overcast, and the light is diffused. The colors have a richness and seem to glow from within. I often try to capture this quality in my work and will choose deep, lush colors set off with sparks of highly contrasting hues.

I prefer natural fabrics, primarily silk and wool, for both piecing and appliqué. Heavy Guatemalan and Japanese cottons also work well. The natural fabrics are much easier to work with than the synthetics. Their drape and hand just cannot be matched by man-made fabrics. For my heavy coats, I work almost exclusively in wool. For my lighter jackets, I often use a lighter wool gabardine as a base and appliqué with silk. I use heavier and suit-weight silks for my lightest-weight jackets.

Appliqué pieces need to hold a crease, so I avoid fabrics like crepe de chine, which

tend to be springy and difficult to manage. Very sheer fabrics, such as China silk, are not suitable, because the base fabric that I stitch them to for stability can be seen through them. For appliqué, shantung silk, silk broadcloth, and Thai silk are the easiest silks to work with; flannel and gabardine are the most cooperative wools.

I pull out piles of fabric, adding and subtracting colors until I'm satisfied with the mix. Certain hues will excite and enhance each other. Sometimes only a dash of color will make an ordinary group of colors come alive. I spend a lot of time testing color combinations by cutting thin strips to mimic the design and laying them out on fabric that approximates the larger areas of color in my design (left photo, page 62).

Proportions of color are critical, but I seldom mark up a full-scale copy of my coat or jacket pattern to use as a guide. To check if I've made one area of color too large or small, such as a front yoke, I cut a piece of

Hyman (above) sketches designs in black and white but prefers to use bits of fabrics laid out on garment fabric to decide on color. At right, zigzags of red appliqué disguise the rectangular shape of Hyman's "Lightning Coat." (Photo by Anthony Rush Ledbetter)

white paper to roughly the size of an area I have in mind; then I hold it up against myself in front of a mirror or pin it to a mannequin. If the proportion is good, I use the paper shape as a guide to cut fabric. My "Lightning Coat," for example, has an area of diagonally striped gray that's narrower than the width between the two sleeve seams; black fabric fills in the rest of the width (see drawing, p. 61). When I was deciding on how large to make the gray area, I wasn't concerned where the sleeve seams fell.

Through a series of mistakes, I've found that a band of light color near the center of the body surrounded by a much darker color is complementary, while the reverse is not. The first scheme makes the wearer seem slim because it turns the viewer's attention away from the body outline. In Chanel-style jackets, a center panel about 10 in. wide seems to work best.

When the color finally works to my satisfaction, I make notes on my original draw-

ing so that I won't forget the order. As I work out the color, I think about which technique I should use. Piecing is much faster than appliqué, so if I can achieve the same design, I choose piecing first. However, appliqué is more versatile, in that it gives one the ability to lay the pieces of fabric anywhere on the garment. In addition, since the appliqué fabric sits on the surface of the base fabric, it creates a unique sense of depth, particularly with thicker fabrics such as wool.

Piecing—After choosing the fabric, I'm ready to construct the garment sections, starting with piecing. Piecing works well if the design has straight lines or rows of squares and rectangles or if it is a geometric design that is based on intersecting vertical and horizontal lines. If the piecing is to have appliqué on top, a very simple design, like a grid or stripes, works best. I generally piece on the crosswise or lengthwise grain

of the fabric, occasionally sewing in a section on the bias. Pieced areas have a tendency to shrink because of all the seams, so I make each pieced section about 1 in. larger on all sides.

It's easier to strip-piece than it is to insert individual pieces, such as squares, into a field of fabric; therefore, I prefer seams to cross the entire width of the garment. Seams have a very strong visual impact, especially if the fabric is a solid color, so I take particular care to place them in such a way that they work with, and enhance, my composition.

The shadows of seams can be very distracting, and they can become unintentional design elements; seam shadows in light-blue fabric, for example, turn into darker blue lines crisscrossing an area. In order to draw attention away from seams, I use colors that are highly contrasting. For example, I might place a red square in a black field with seams running the entire

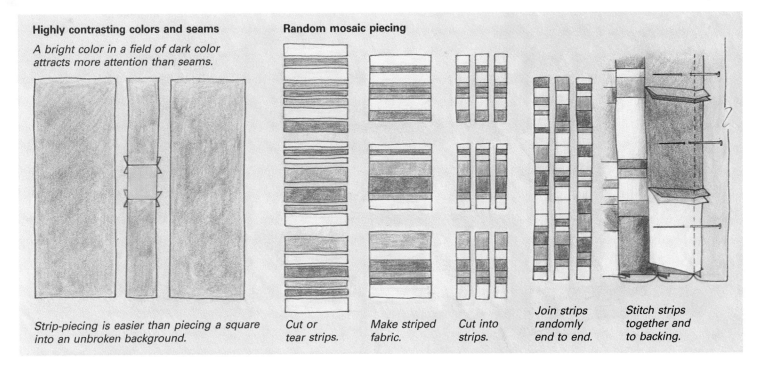

Highly contrasting colors and seams

A bright color in a field of dark color attracts more attention than seams.

Strip-piecing is easier than piecing a square into an unbroken background.

Random mosaic piecing

Cut or tear strips.

Make striped fabric.

Cut into strips.

Join strips randomly end to end.

Stitch strips together and to backing.

Hyman divided each half of this jacket front into two vertical panels. Each panel top is mosaic piecing; the bottom is a solid color. (Photo by Anthony Rush Ledbetter)

width and length of the black fabric (drawing at left, above).

Before I begin to piece, I trace at least part of my design on paper at full scale. When I've finalized the measurements for each piece, I add ¼-in. seam allowances to each interior piece and ⅜-in. allowances if the fabric ravels. I never add wider allowances to inside pieces, as many of my designs are intricate, and wide seams would add bulk. If part of the piecing falls in a garment seam, I add a ½-in. seam allowance.

If my design consists of a series of identical units, I use the Seminole piecing technique. I tear tightly woven fabric into strips from selvage to selvage; a rotary cutter works better for loose fabrics. I sew the strips side by side to form stripes. Using the rotary cutter, I then cut perpendicularly across the stripes to make a series of identical pieced strips. I join these with other pieced strips, thus forming the composition. After stitching a pair of strips together, I iron the seam.

If I'm piecing lines that intersect—a grid, for example—I break down the design vertically so I can sew the longest lines in the composition as one continuous seam, which will look straighter and smoother than continuous horizontal seams.

Another kind of piecing that I use creates a rich mosaic of small squares and rectangles (photo at left). I sew many fabric strips (¾ in. to 2½ in. wide) together into stripes and then cut across the stripes to make narrow pieced strips. Next, I randomly join the pieced strips end to end to form longer strips, which I sew, right sides together, onto a fabric backing, stitching through all three layers at once (drawing at right, above). I've been using a high-count (tightly woven) polyester/cotton for backing thin fabric, like silk. The backing also serves to smoothly finish the inside surface of the piecing.

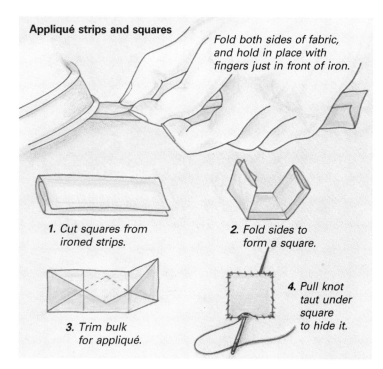

Appliqué strips and squares

Fold both sides of fabric, and hold in place with fingers just in front of iron.

1. Cut squares from ironed strips.

2. Fold sides to form a square.

3. Trim bulk for appliqué.

4. Pull knot taut under square to hide it.

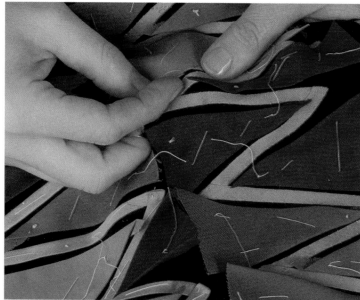

Only a tiny bit of thread is visible on the surface of the pieces that Hyman appliqués to the base with a slipstitch. All of the pieces are basted in place with their seam allowances pressed under.

Appliqué—Next, I move on to the appliqué. I prefer to appliqué on the smaller sections of the garment before I assemble them. I do all my appliqué by hand because I don't like the look of machine satin stitch.

All the edges of appliqué pieces need at least a ⅛-in. seam allowance; I prefer to iron the edges under before I lay out my design so I'm working with actual-size pieces. Using a rotary cutter, I cut long, narrow bias strips three times the finished width; sometimes the strips are only ³⁄₁₆ in. wide when finished. Bias strips can be sewn to the base fabric in any direction without puckering. Because bias will stretch, I don't pull it too tight when I sew it down; otherwise, it will cause the base fabric to pucker. I iron under the bias-strip edges so they'll be three layers deep. My Rowenta iron has a very accurate steam control. I can iron very close to my fingers without excess steam escaping and burning them (drawing above). For small squares—½ in. or less—I iron under two sides of a long strip that I cut on-grain, I cut that strip into small sections, and then I iron under the two raw edges to form a square. I trim off as much of the excess bulk as possible, since the squares are now nine layers thick. On larger squares and triangles, I iron under the seams about ¼ in. or so.

To arrange the appliqué strips, I work with the base fabric pinned on a wall so I can lay out the design vertically, the way it will be seen when it's worn. I pin the pieces onto the base fabric. Sometimes the smaller squares are hard to work with because the seams pop out, so I often cut out the exact-sized squares from a single layer of the same fabric and use them in place of the ironed pieces. The small squares are so light that they stick to the garment without pins. Later, I substitute the actual pieces that will be sewn into place.

I enjoy this part of the process because there are still many design decisions to be made. Sometimes I change parts of the design or find that a color isn't working. When everything is in place, I work on something else so I can return with fresh eyes.

After all the parts of the composition are pinned and ready to go, it's time to baste. I repin everything so I can take it off the wall without disrupting the design. I remove the entire section and lay it on the table. The pieces have to be basted because the pins would fall out during handling. If there are any appliqué pieces that cross over a seam, I baste them up to the seamline and leave them dangling; I sew them down after I sew the garment seams together.

When I've completed all the basting, I slipstitch each piece to the base, using thread that's slightly darker than the appliqué (photo above). I make my stitches about ³⁄₁₆ in. apart, being careful not to pull them too tight, or the piece will pucker. I make several stitches close together at the corners to keep the seams from popping out, as well as to secure the piece.

Points on triangles are harder to handle. I sew up one side, fold down the point, and trim off excess fabric. Using the needle tip, I stuff the seams under the fabric and hold everything in place with my left thumbnail. I then make several tiny stitches and continue to sew down the remaining side.

Inside curves need to be clipped before they can be turned under. I make extra stitches at clipped points so everything will be well secured. If a corner feels bulky, I trim off excess fabric from the back seam. I don't do this if the fabric is light and the extra layers aren't noticeable.

I line most garments, so I leave the knots on the back side. If I don't plan to line a garment or attach the lining, I hide the knots under the appliqué by making the knot

just under one edge of the appliqué and pulling the thread out on the opposite side.

Only after all the appliqué is finished is each garment piece ready to be pressed. If a piece is puckering, I stretch it out flat, right side down, and pin it to my ironing board—a 30-in. x 50-in. piece of Masonite covered with padding and cotton drill. I steam-press each appliqué in place. When it's cool, I turn it over, pin it down if necessary, and press the front, using a press cloth.

Finishing—The garment is now ready for final construction. I use interfacing to add body, to act as a buffer between bulky seams and the lining, and to reinforce areas with pieces that run off-grain. I use Hymo hair canvas for wools or polyester/cotton. If there are many layers of piecing, sometimes interfacing isn't needed. I sew the interfacing into the collar, shoulders, and front around the outside edges. I don't use pad stitches.

When I'm sewing all the parts together, I sometimes find it difficult to get the thick appliquéd and pieced sections to lay flat and neat. I do a lot of internal trimming and grading. I also use a lot of pressing equipment—a clapper, a ham, and a press cloth. After I sew the seams together, I finish appliquéing any pieces that cross over seams and have been left dangling.

I like linings—they hide messy insides, they're easier to do than finishing seams, they add warmth, and they make slipping on a garment easy. If I want a piece to be light or sheer, I use French seams and no lining. I also use bindings to finish off the edges. ☐

Ann Williamson Hyman's work is shown at Julie: Artisans' Gallery in New York City and at Obiko in San Francisco, CA. Hyman teaches contemporary quilting and art-to-wear classes at the Oregon School of Arts and Crafts in Portland, OR.

Mastering the Art of Hand Appliqué

The legacy of the Baltimore Friendship Quilts

by Colette Wolff

hand appliqué, a skill once routinely taught young women, is the seemingly simple task of sewing small pieces of fabric to a larger background. But perfect execution, in the manner of our finest historical examples, takes dexterity, practice, and much patience. Nonetheless, hand appliqué is a learnable skill, and the procedures have not changed since the mid-1800s, when the Baltimore Friendship Quilts (see page 68) were made.

Beginning with a design drawn full-size on paper, a set of paper patterns—one pattern for each element within the design—is traced and cut. Cardboard templates that can survive repeated tracings are made for paper patterns that will be duplicated many times. Appliqué patterns and templates do not include seam allowances. Seam allowances are added when the fabric appliqués are cut.

Patterns are traced onto the right side of the chosen fabric with a pin-sharp pencil. For seam allowance, each appliqué is cut 1/8 in. to 1/4 in., depending on its size, *outside* that penciled outline. This seam allowance will be turned under when the appliqué is stitched to the background fabric. Slipstitches, closely spaced and nearly invisible, secure the appliqués to the background fabric.

Let's follow the development of a simple appliqué design (see photo, page 66) from pattern to completion. Grain lines on the larger pattern pieces in drawing 1 on page 66 correspond to the straight weave of the foundation fabric over which the appliqué

will be stitched. Grain matching isn't necessary for small appliqués or when cutting an appliqué from printed fabric requires special positioning on the pattern. However, it's a precaution against buckling for the larger ones.

The sample design is stitched to a block meant to finish 12 in. sq. Since the necessary seam allowances aren't included in that measurement, the background fabric is cut 13 in. by 13 in. to include 1/2-in. seam allowances all around. With the master drawing pinned underneath the background fabric, the design is traced onto the right side of the square. Placing the design and fabric over a light box or in front of a window during the day helps expose the outlines.

The outlines penciled on the background fabric and each appliqué should be just obvious enough to follow while you're working. You need them to duplicate the original design and keep the appliqués and the background in proper form, but they're objectionable afterward.

When appliqués are sewn with the tiny slipstitches favored by those Baltimore ladies, the only thread visible on the surface emerges to catch a tiny sliver of the appliqué on the fold before disappearing directly into the background fabric against the appliqué's edge (see drawing 2, page 66). The thread moves forward from one stitch to the next in back, never in front. Worked with a single thread colored to blend into the appliqué fabric, fine slipstitches, 1/16 in. to 3/16 in. long, are almost invisible when the thread is drawn taut. Beginning knots and securing stitches that end a seam should be trapped behind the appliqué. If it's pos-

Wolff finger-creases the edge of an appliqué.

Procedures for making this appliqué sampler are given in the drawings below.

sible to pry up the edge of an appliqué with a fingernail, the stitches are too far apart, or the thread tension is too loose. On the other hand, if the sewing thread is pulled too tight, the piece will pucker and begin to shrink.

An appliqué design is executed backward. "Background elements first, foreground last" is the rule that determines progression. In our design the four-lobed figure, or quatrefoil, appears to be behind both leaves and the flower; one leaf interrupts the shape of another leaf, and the flower covers sections of two leaves and the quatrefoil. Stitching proceeds from the quatrefoil to leaf A, then B and C, and finishes with the flower patterns D, E, F, and G, in that order. Where one appliqué covers the unturned seam allowance of another, the stitching of the appliqué on top will catch and hold the appliqué beneath. One seam functions for two when the rule is followed.

The quatrefoil doesn't have a pattern, because, for appliqué, lines that curve or meander are formed from bias tape bent as it is being applied to follow the shape of the design. For the ½-in.-wide quatrefoil in our design, a 1-in.-wide strip of bias fabric is cut, and ¼-in. seam allowances on either side are pressed underneath. With two single threaded needles, one for each side of the tape, the outer contour of a curve or point is stitched down first, followed by the inside curve or angle with the second

1. Making the pattern pieces
Starting with a design drawn full size on paper, trace and cut pattern pieces for each element. The quatrefoil will be made from a bias strip, so it has no pattern. Mark grain lines on the larger pattern pieces so the grains of the appliqué and background fabric will align.

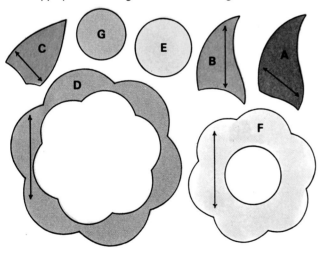

2. Slipstitching an appliqué
To slipstitch an appliqué, bring the needle up through the background fabric, catch just the edge of the appliqué, and then stick the needle back through the background fabric. Move the needle forward to the next stitch behind the work.

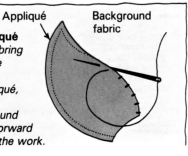

3. Stitching bias tape
Stitch bias tape with two needles, one for each side. To turn a corner, first secure the point with a tacking stitch. Then redirect the tape and sew for ½ in. or so beyond the point. At the inner angle, pinch excess fabric into a fold and catch it at the notch with a stitch. Finally, push the excess fabric underneath with the needle and tack the opening closed.

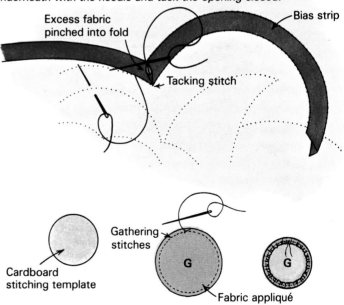

4. Forming round or oval appliqués
For round or oval appliqués, trace and cut a thin cardboard stitching template from the paper pattern. Straight-stitch around the edge of the fabric appliqué, within the seam allowance. Center the template over the wrong side of the fabric appliqué, and pull the stitching thread to gather the seam allowance evenly over the template. Then cut and pry out the template.

needle. Gentle stretching of the outside edge of the bias strip permits its inner edge to contract into a smaller arc. At corners, the tip is secured first with an extra tacking stitch. After the bias tape is redirected, sewing continues for ½ in. or so beyond the point. At the inside angle, excess tape is pinched into a fold and caught at the notch with a stitch (see drawing 3, page 66). The fold is then pushed underneath the tape and discreetly tacked.

Some appliquers first turn and baste seam allowances behind each appliqué and then baste the appliqués in place on the foundation fabric before beginning to slipstitch. But most appliqué can be done without the extra work of the first step. After the penciled outline on the appliqué is carefully matched to the corresponding outline on the background fabric, the appliqué is pinned in place or basted if pins will be in the way. Stab-pinning—sticking a pin through the outline on the appliqué and then through the exact corresponding point on the background outline—will position an appliqué accurately. With a short length of the seam allowance turned under ahead of the needle, the appliqué is finger-creased on the penciled line, and the edge of the fold is then slipstitched to the foundation. Stitching proceeds in this manner, pinch-creasing, stitching, pinch-creasing, and stitching again, until the appliqué is seamed in place. (Appliquers insist on us-

By multiplying and varying the size of simple elements, Wolff creates an elaborate appliqué block.

5. Stitching the appliqué

Prepare curved edges by clipping fabric almost to penciled line. Trim points to eliminate excess seam allowance. Stitch one side of appliqué up to the point, turning under and finger-creasing seam allowance as you proceed. Use needle to push under seam allowance on other side. At base of leaf, seam allowance isn't turned under or slipstitched, because it will be covered by appliqué B. A longer edge can be basted down.

After you've stitched leaves A, B, and C, prepare and sew appliqué D. Clip seam allowances around outside edge. Baste inside edge of appliqué D and edge of appliqué E to background fabric, as they'll be covered by appliqué F. Notch inside and outside edges of appliqué F, as both will be slipstitched.

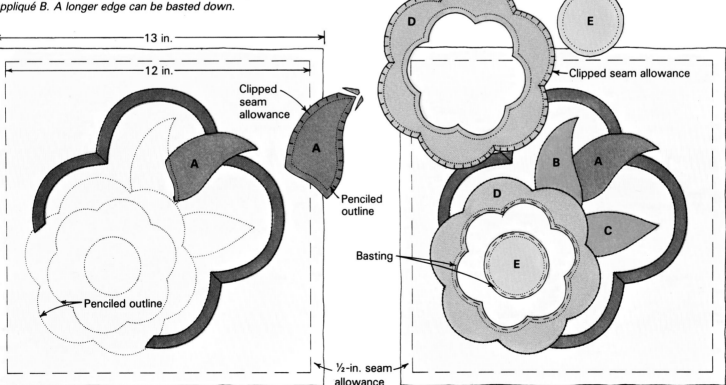

ing 100% cotton fabrics because they retain a crease.) The needle's tip is used to urge reluctant seam allowances beneath and to finesse curves into scrupulous alignment. When an appliqué is folded exactly on the penciled line, it assumes the shape it's supposed to have, and the penciled line disappears into the fold. If the appliqué was carefully pinned or basted to its site within the design, the stitched edge of the appliqué conforms to, and covers, the line on the background.

However, on all but straight-edged appliqués, seam allowances won't lay flat without prior preparation. At inside angles, the seam allowance must be clipped right up to the penciled line. On inside curves, seam allowances should be cut at intervals and snipped almost to, but not quite up to, the penciled line. The steeper the curve, the closer the clips must be spaced. Outside curves are treated like inside curves.

If circles and ovals are preformed over stitching templates, which are simply extra cardboard templates cut from the patterns, distortion can be avoided. After plain sewing around the appliqué inside the seam allowance is completed, the appliqué is gathered snugly and evenly over the centered template. The template is then cut and pried from inside the appliqué, and the appliqué is slipstitched to the design (see drawing 4, page 66).

Meticulous points, the ultimate test of an appliquer's technique, come with practice. Sewing them precisely and cleanly, with all seam-allowance threads safely tucked away, makes fingers into thumbs and needles into clumsy tools, especially when the points are slender. Where feasible, cut the appliqué so seam allowances at the point fall on the bias. It's essential to taper seam allowances into the penciled line at the tip and trim straight across just above the point. Stitch up to the point on one side; then, using the needle, tease and shove the seam allowances at the tip and on the other side underneath the appliqué. Since seam allowances on either side of the point are often only several threads of the fabric wide, stitching at the point must be 1/16 in. apart or closer.

To appliqué at the level of excellence apparent in a Baltimore Friendship Quilt, perfection is the goal. Impeccable hand appliqué is free of puckers and wrinkles. Background fabric measurements are the same at the finish as they were at the beginning. The appliquéd design duplicates the original drawing with curves that flow smoothly, circles that are truly round, and points that are sharp. To eliminate unnecessary seams, the design is sequentially appliquéd. Each appliqué, with seam allowances confined underneath, is securely attached to the background fabric with slip stitches that are regular and visible only upon close inspection. The mechanics of the appliqué process (pencil lines, basting, tails of sewing thread, threads from seam

allowances) are invisible when the appliqué is finished.

Flawless appliqué also depends on designing that doesn't ask more of the medium than it can deliver. Since seam allowances are essential for slipstitched appliqué, the surface of an appliqué at any given cross section must be wide enough to cover the seam allowances that are folded beneath. Therefore, dots and thin lines are impossible, and long, skinny shapes that narrow to a point are difficult. Because of the obligatory turned edge, figures with busy, convoluted contours and bitsy shapes are frustrating or unworkable.

We can be grateful to the creators of the Baltimore Friendship Quilts for the gift of their theme. Flowers and foliage stylize readily into streamlined shapes that adapt to the limitations of hand appliqué and, most important, beg for exploration of all the fabric colors and textures in the marketplace. Before being appliquéd, two fabrics can be pieced together with a straight or curving seam, at the spine of a leaf, for example, to give additional definition by the color change. Layering, the process of sewing one appliqué over another with each one smaller than the one before, introduces successive colors within a pattern. Reverse appliqué, slashing and cutting holes inside an appliqué before turning and stitching down these interior seam allowances, exposes the fabric color underneath the top appliqué as another outlined shape.

Needleworkers who feel intimidated at the word *design* can't plead unfamiliarity or inability to draw when the subject is a floral. Doodling with lines, circles, and ovals can be the start of a design. Coins, cutouts from magazines, and household objects can be used as tracing templates. A single floral element, multiplied and perhaps varied in size, can be developed into clusters of blossoms or buds on a twining vine, as illustrated by the design on page 67. As demonstrated in the Baltimore Friendship Quilts, accompaniments such as birds, bows, butterflies, books, containers, and trellises, traced from a printed source if need be, complement a floral composition.

A floral design for appliqué doesn't have to be elaborate to be effective. We're not competing with our historical counterparts to determine who can spend the longest time doing the most ambitious appliqué. It's quality that communicates, not quantity by itself, just as it's the artistry gracing the designs and guiding the stitchery in a Baltimore Friendship Quilt that excites our admiration, not the hours and patience required for execution. In the spirit of here and now, reflecting our personal joys and concerns, we can create unique floral appliqué equal in loveliness and craft to the best created in the past.

Colette Wolff runs a needlework-design business called Platypus from her home in New York City. Illustrations by the author.

The Baltimore Friendship Quilt

During the mid-1800s, expert needlewomen in the vicinity of Baltimore created an extraordinary group of appliquéd bedcovers known today as the Baltimore Friendship Quilts. Pictorially they celebrate flowers and foliage with a scattering of birds, bows, bibles, musical instruments, and occasionally an American flag for variety and significance. But that description doesn't begin to convey the impact of the finest of these quilts. Each is a splendid affirmation of life, all the more astonishing because it is a textile painstakingly constructed from hundreds of cutouts of colored cloth fastened with thousands of minute stitches to squares of plain background fabric. Those anonymous Baltimore ladies, out of their need to make beauty and order into something tangible and lasting, left a legacy of inspiration to which generations of quiltmakers have responded.

The floral theme of a Baltimore Friendship Quilt is universally familiar, but its manner of expression reflects the quiet pace, gracious style, and conventional spirit of an earlier period and society. The detail, delicacy, complexity, formality, small scale, and colors of the designs within each quilt—flowers and foliage arranged in wreaths, sprays and bouquets that overflow baskets, vases, and cornucopias—indicate an imagination making the most of the available visual and material resources.

Designs from these quilts have been, and continue to be, faithfully copied. Yet another kind of response interprets, rather than imitates, accepting past glories as a trust to be continued with beautiful floral appliqués that record our sensibilities today. Boldness, freedom, informality, openness, asymmetry, and the use of contrast between large and small, light and dark, near and far, describe a 20th-century approach to design. In addition to the Baltimore quilts themselves, influences such as impressionist paintings, glossy seed catalogs, advertising art, flowers unknown to

One of the finest historical examples of appliqué is this Baltimore Friendship Quilt, which was made around 1850. The consistency of the design and stitching of this particular quilt indicates that it may have been executed by just one woman, although quilts of this style were frequently worked by many hands. Photo courtesy of the Metropolitan Museum of Art, Sansbury Mills Fund, 1974.

those Baltimore ladies, colors that they did not have in their fabric palettes, and a liberal attitude toward fabric itself are all evident in contemporary floral appliqué.

A Baltimore Friendship Quilt challenges the artist in anyone whose fingers itch at the sight of superb appliqué. But is it possible for one person to design and stitch such a floral statement? Although the evidence is circumstantial rather than factual, recent research indicates that one woman, supported by a group, was the major creative force behind many definitive examples of these quilts. If this conclusion is true, was she more accomplished than we can expect ourselves to be? Our needle artist from long ago probably received genteel instruction in the skills considered necessary for a girl to attract a husband, among which fancy needlework and renderings on paper would be important. As a designer, she would have relied primarily on instinct and observation, qualities that any one of us can match and surpass if we add the considerable means at our disposal. Since she undoubtedly began sewing when she was very young, she had a head start on most of us in that regard, but appliqué skills can be mastered with guidance and some practice, allowing us to catch up quickly. —Colette Wolff ☐

Shapely Curves

Machine-stitching curved pieces opens a soft-edged world to the quilter

by Janice Anthony

the ability to piece curves on a sewing machine gives the quiltmaker the advantages of major quiltmaking traditions—patchwork and appliqué—and the chance to follow the imagination into new regions. Patchwork is fast, as the straight lines of the geometric shapes lend themselves to machine piecing, while appliqué allows for complex designs with the grace and natural flow of curves, though the pieces are usually small, and the designs complicated. Machine-stitching curved pieces gives me the best of both traditions and the opportunity to use large spaces and long, flowing lines.

The difficulty in piecing curves is that one edge is convex and one is concave, so when the pieces are right sides together for stitching, they don't easily line up. The quiltmaker has to coax them into alignment. But with accurate cutting and marking and careful stitching, it can be done.

Designing with curves opens up a wide range of inspirational sources, from the cosmos to earthly landscapes. Mountains, rivers, cloud formations, wandering roads—visible landscapes alone could furnish an endless series of quilt designs. And within the landscape, especially flowers and foliage, are myriad sources of images using curved pieces.

Making the pattern—After I sketch my final design, I redraw it on a sheet of drawing paper. Then, to develop the colors, I tape tracing paper over the sketch and fill

From *Threads* magazine (June 1987) 11:30-32

"A curve is the nicest distance between two points."—Mae West

in the sections, using colored pencil. This colored sketch will also help me during the stitching to identify the pieces and their places in the design. By coloring only the tracing, I leave the original drawing clean for patternmaking, and it's easy to change if the colored rendering shows a section that doesn't work successfully. Tracing paper erases more easily than drawing paper, and my drawings usually need to be erased several times.

Next, I enlarge the design to its full size and draw it on paper. Eventually I'll cut apart the full-size pattern on the design lines and use each piece as a pattern for cutting out the fabric. The simplest way to transfer the design to full size is to use an opaque projector, but transferring it with a grid system can be done in an afternoon.

To do this, I lay a reusable piece of graph tracing paper with a ½-in. grid (available from art-supply stores) over the sketch. I then rule paper that is slightly larger than the full size of the quilt into a grid with the same number of squares as the grid covering the original design, but with each square proportionately larger. For example, if a 4-in. by 6-in. sketch is to become a 24-in. by 36-in. hanging, I rule the large sheet at 6-in. intervals. In addition, I lightly rule the large grid at halfway intervals. A 1-in. margin around the outer edges allows for uneven piecing and a final seam allowance. For the full-size pattern, pieces of freezer paper or large sheets of drawing paper can be taped together. Although this isn't very convenient, the resulting squared-off lines can halve the time spent ruling. The ideal solution is to use a roll of paper 36 in. wide and seemingly infinitely long, sold by paper companies. I streamline the enlarging process by judiciously cropping or expanding my original sketch until its measurements are whole numbers so they can be multiplied easily.

Then, square by square, I transfer the small sketch to the large paper. This can

The sweeping curves of Janice Anthony's quilts are machine- and hand-pieced and hand-quilted. Facing page: "Polyphony," 1987; 46 in. by 65 in.; cotton, painted with fiber-reactive dyes. Detail below. Photos by author.

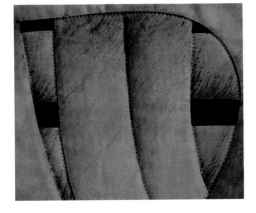

be difficult. Tricks include counting squares to correlate them and marking off halfway points, especially if the piece is to be enlarged more than four times. Once a general outline appears on the full-size drawing, I critique it to see how the design has translated, where transference was inaccurate, and where areas and lines can be improved.

Since the full-size pattern will eventually be cut apart on the design lines, it needs landmarks for cutting and piecing. Referring to the original color sketch, I write on each pattern piece the color fabric it is to be cut from, differentiating between shades and sometimes matching them to a swatch chart. Once the pieces have been cut apart, the only way to remind oneself where they belong would be to reassemble them like a puzzle, so the colors must be marked accurately. If the design is especially complicated, the pieces can be numbered or labeled and keyed to the original color sketch.

Each pattern piece also needs notches so the seam edges can be lined up for stitching. Notches are the little V's marked on the seam lines of the pattern pieces and cut outward on the fabric pieces. On a straight seam, accurately cut ends and corners serve as unstated notches. For a lengthy curved seam, however, notches on both adjoining edges are essential markers of points where the pieces of fabric must meet.

I mark gentle curves at regular intervals—no further the 6 in. apart—by drawing diamonds on the lines of the pattern, as shown in drawing A, page 72. I mark tighter curves and curves that change direction, such as S-curves and undulating lines, more closely. I sometimes have to finish stitching particularly tight curves by hand after I have sewn as far as possible with the machine. I mark these areas also. For clarity, the notches can be numbered.

I then cut the pattern into its separate pieces and pin them to the fabrics for cutting (drawing B). I align the grid lines with the fabric grain so that the grain is uniform across the finished quilt. The outer edge of each paper pattern piece is the seam line. When cutting, I leave a ½-in. seam allowance and trim it to ¼ in. after I've sewn all the seams. The cutting line can also be marked, but training the eye to cut uniform allowances is faster. I cut outward V's in the fabric, aligned with each notch in the pattern. For greater accuracy, I later mark the notches right at the seam line with an erasable pencil.

Sewing—Beginning at the center of the design, I pin and sew the pieces together one at a time. With the pieces right sides together, I align the notches and pin through the exact center of each notch drawn on the seam line (drawing C). A gentle curve should lie fairly smoothly, with the convex seam allowance ruffling slightly and the concave edge pulling slightly. With a more pronounced curve, I often have to clip ¼ in. into the concave seam allowance, at approximately 1-in. intervals. I pin tighter curves at closer intervals, pulling the concave edge slightly to align the notches.

I begin machine-sewing the more gentle curves, rather than the tight or S-curves. Where several small pieces join a big piece, I first sew the small pieces into a larger unit. I make about 12 stitches per inch. This prevents the numerous needle-holes created by shorter stitches and facilitates any ripping out that may be necessary. When possible, I sew with the concave edge on top of the convex edge, as this edge tends to creep in, and when it's on top, I can see and control it. I pull both pieces slightly, as when easing a seam in dressmaking. If there is more than a ⅛-in. discrepancy between notches, I go back to the pattern to see if I made a mistake in cutting or marking.

Difficult curves are S-shapes, those with a tightly curved area between straighter lines, and those that become progressively tighter. I sew a tight curve by matching the notches, clipping the inner curve to ¼ in. from the seam line, and then sewing out from the center of the curve in each direction (drawing D). Next, I sew the straighter sections, continuing out from the center. A progressively tighter curve should be carefully clipped where there's too much pull and should be sewn from the gentler end toward the tighter end. An S-curve can be sewn from one end to the other, but it is easier to sew each curve separately, out from the point at which the curves change direction. Whenever the presser foot begins to take up more space than the fabric will allow, I iron the rest of the seam line in place and handsew.

I handle particularly recalcitrant curves, or those that are too tight for the machine's presser foot, by carefully clipping the concave edge, pressing it to the underside, and handsewing in place (drawing E). To eliminate extra bulk, I trim the seam allowance to ¼ in. before sewing, I place this piece over the adjoining piece, and I pin it in place, aligning the points at which the notches appear on the paper pattern. Then I blindstitch by hand.

To make sure they lie flat, I iron the sections I've sewn. I clip the concave curves and iron both seam allowances toward the piece that I want to appear to advance toward the viewer. To check for accuracy of the stitching, I lay the pattern pieces on top of the sewn pieces. The notches on the unsewn edges of the fabric should still match the notches on the pattern, and stitched seam lines should run underneath the line where the pattern pieces abut.

Ironing may show up some of the possible problems. If the outer surface of the

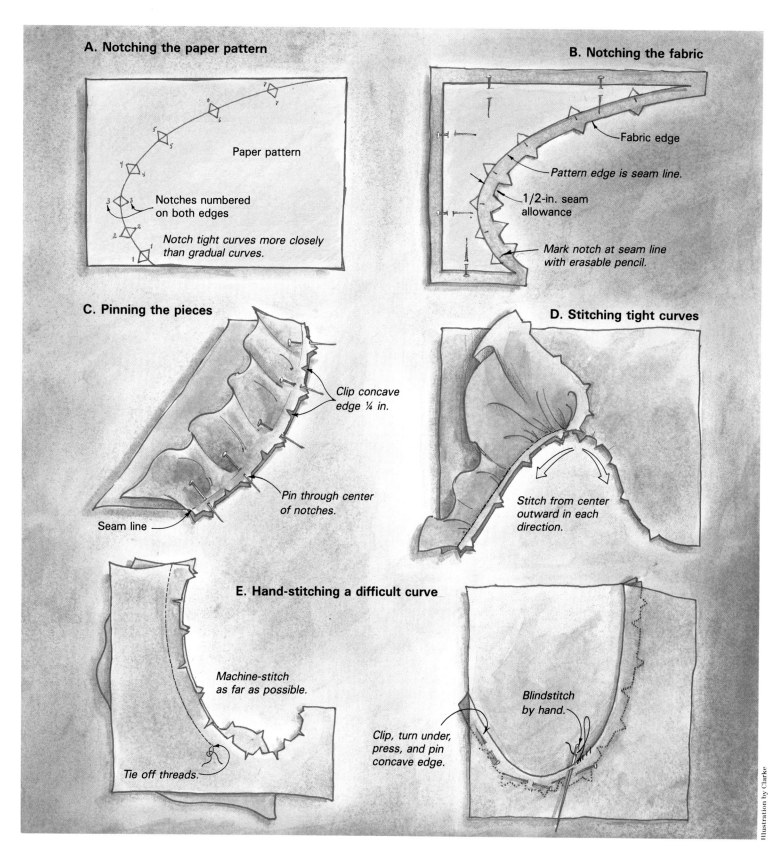

A. Notching the paper pattern

Paper pattern

Notches numbered
on both edges

Notch tight curves more closely
than gradual curves.

B. Notching the fabric

Fabric edge

Pattern edge is seam line.

1/2-in. seam
allowance

Mark notch at seam line
with erasable pencil.

C. Pinning the pieces

Clip concave
edge ¼ in.

Pin through center
of notches.

Seam line

D. Stitching tight curves

Stitch from center
outward in each
direction.

E. Hand-stitching a difficult curve

Machine-stitch
as far as possible.

Tie off threads.

Clip, turn under,
press, and pin
concave edge.

Blindstitch
by hand.

Illustration by Clarke

fabric has a fold ironed in, this may indicate that I sewed the seam allowance a little bit too narrow. If I find that it's impossible to iron it away without causing the whole piece to ripple, I resew on the ironed fold line. If this new seam line is more than ⅛ in. from the first, however, I recheck against the pattern.

When ironing, I sometimes find that one of the two pieces of fabric has a slight bulge or ripple along the seam line. If it is the piece with the convex edge of the seam, the concave seam may be too tight, and I

can relax it by carefully clipping the seam allowance. If the piece with the concave edge ripples or bulges, I have to take it apart and resew it.

To allow for adjustments, I usually trim the seam allowances to ¼ in. only after I've pieced the whole top. As with any pieced quilt, some areas may bulge up slightly when the entire work is ironed and laid out. Although precision in cutting, pinning, and sewing makes this occur surprisingly infrequently, a wide seam allowance leaves latitude for correction.

Though I have emphasized the need for accuracy, it is actually no more necessary than accuracy in sewing geometric pieces. Machine-piecing a quilt with curved lines clearly speeds up the work. The freshness and beauty of designs that can be made with curved lines should encourage quiltmakers to be more adventurous with this technique, making new discoveries and unforgettable quilts. □

Janice Anthony is an artist and a quiltmaker in Brooks, ME.

Fabric Puzzles

Inlay your pieces for a freewheeling quilt

by Ellen Oppenheimer

*a*s I go through the creative process of designing and constructing quilts, I often follow two precepts that are helpful in developing the work. The first is: Image develops process. I try to look at ideas and then develop the techniques to realize them. The second guideline that I find helpful and use often is: Just try it. It is difficult to try something new, different, and unexplored. To help myself embark on things that possibly might not work out, I remind myself that the materials that I am using are not woven of golden threads. Most of the yardage costs a few dollars a yard and if I make a mistake, a smaller piece or a different patch will have to serve.

A good example of a technique that developed from an idea is machine inlaying, a method of piecing I now use extensively. I had made a rough sketch for "Untitled Quilt," which is shown in the photo at right. I loved the drawing, but I could not conceive of how to put it together. Until that time I had only pieced squares together; I tried to plot out how I could stitch the pieces together as if I were creating a mosaic and realized it was impossible. Hand appliqué was entirely out of the question because I wanted to use machine stitching as much as possible, and I didn't like the look of machine appliqué. The result was the first version of machine inlaying, which I've been polishing ever since.

A closer look at the accurate fitting around the curves of the yellow dots (near left) reveals what is possible using the machine-inlaying technique described in this article. A dazzling combination of fabrics and piecing, Ellen Oppenheimer's quilt "Pyrotechnics" (far left) is almost entirely machine stitched.

Inlaying fabric with machine-stitched seams cuts down the layers associated with appliqué. In her 1986 "Untitled Quilt" (right), Oppenheimer inlayed the straight, black-striped yellow fabric into the black-and-yellow central fabric, and the yellow squares into the blue and black border.

Machine inlaying makes crisp lines, as shown in the detailed photo at left, and keeps the layers of fabric to a minimum. It's good for odd shapes, whether they're straight-sided or curved. I hope that it will prove useful and interesting to other quilters, and to garment designers as well. In both crafts and fine art, the materials always stand between the artist's thought and the viewer's perception. The more skillful you are with your materials, the better chance you have of communicating your ideas.

No guessing with a tracing

I usually start with a rough drawing. Besides having a drawing, I often select a background fabric, lay it on my table, and

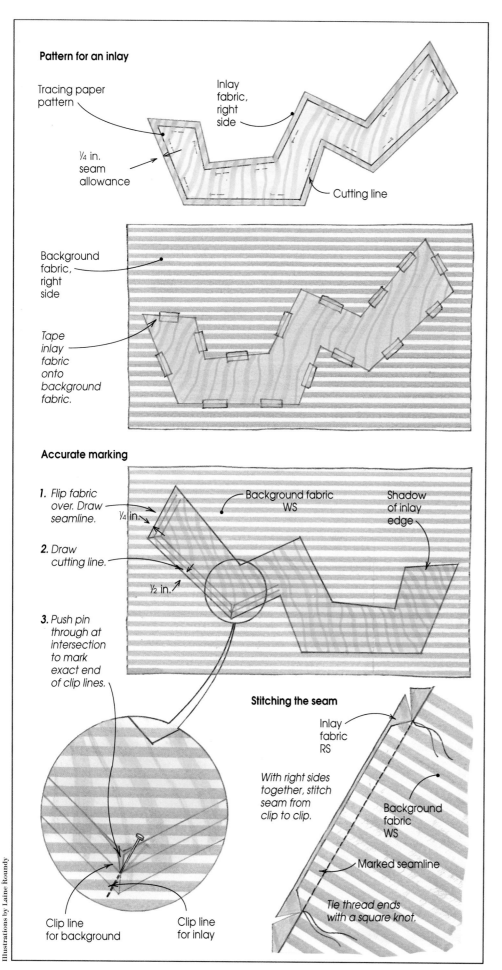

Pattern for an inlay

Tracing paper pattern

Inlay fabric, right side

¼ in. seam allowance

Cutting line

Background fabric, right side

Tape inlay fabric onto background fabric.

Accurate marking

1. Flip fabric over. Draw seamline.

¼ in.

2. Draw cutting line.

½ in.

3. Push pin through at intersection to mark exact end of clip lines.

Background fabric WS

Shadow of inlay edge

Clip line for background

Clip line for inlay

Stitching the seam

Inlay fabric RS

With right sides together, stitch seam from clip to clip.

Background fabric WS

Marked seamline

Tie thread ends with a square knot.

Illustrations by Laine Roundy

place shapes of inlay fabric on top to see what they are going to look like. If everything looks approximately right, I trace the inlay shape I want onto tracing paper or cut a shape freehand. (I buy 3-ft. wide tracing paper from a nearby art supply store.) Then I pin the tracing paper to the right side of the inlay fabric, add ¼ in. seam allowances on straight edges and ½ in. on curved edges, and cut out the fabric shape, as shown in the drawing at left, top.

Tape the inlay to the background with the right sides of both fabrics facing up but leave all corners free, as shown in the second drawing from the top at left; you'll clip at the corners and tape would get in the way. The tape keeps the piece from flopping around. Use magic or non-stick translucent tape. Be careful not to melt the tape with the iron as you work.

If you're working on something large, like a quilt, all that fabric can be unwieldy. A trick I use to keep the fabric flat is to cover my 8-ft. sq. table with flannel taped tightly down; when I lay the quilt on top, the fabric doesn't slide. The flannel also turns the table into a huge ironing board.

A new quilting tool

For the next step, you'll need the equivalent of a light table so you can see the shadow of the inlay from the back of the background fabric. Photographers use a light table, which is a sheet of glass over a light source, to view slides. I started using a light table when I was making "Pyrotechnics," (photo on page 76). I wanted to piece triangles along the edges of 2-in. diameter circles. The pieces had to match the curve of the circles exactly to look realistic; I couldn't get that degree of match unless I traced the circular shape onto the inlay fabric using the light table, and then pieced it precisely into the background fabric. It was to be a very fussy and challenging bit of sewing.

There is no need to buy a fancy commercial light table. My table consists of a pane of frosted glass laid over a box with a fluorescent light tube inside; an incandescent light gets too hot. You can also make a light table surface from a pane of acrylic plastic laid over two 2x4s and a fluorescent tube.

Flip the taped fabric layers over so the reverse side of the background fabric faces up, and place the fabric on the light table. The outline of the inlay fabric will be visible through the background fabric, as shown in the third drawing from the top at left. With a clear ruler, like a C-Thru, and a pencil, draw a line ¼ in. inside the outline; this will be the sewing line. Draw a second line that is ½ in. from the inlay outline; this will be the cutting line for the background fabric.

Although I cut and stitch one side of an

inlay at a time, I need to know where the corners will be, so I also draw the connecting seam and cutting lines. If all the seam and cutting lines of an inlay were marked at once, by the time you were ready to stitch the last seam, the lines would no longer match. The shift happens because some fabric is taken up by the fold of a seam allowance. It's hard to predict how much the turn of the cloth absorbs, so I just work on one line at a time.

Precise intersections

At each corner or intersection, you'll need to clip the seam allowances so they can be sewn and ironed open or to one side. The clips have to line up exactly or there will be gaps or puckers.

The clip in the background fabric extends from the intersection of the cutting lines to the intersections of the seamlines. Draw a pencil line, as shown in the drawing at lower left, facing page, at both ends of the line you're working on.

Push a pin through both fabric layers, from back to front, at the intersections of the seamlines. Turn the fabric with the pin in place so you can see the pin's point. Clip the inlay from the corner to the pin, as shown in the bottom left drawing on the facing page.

Flip the fabric so the back faces up. To start the cut in the back, slip a finger between the two layers, pinch the background fabric, and snip on the cutting line. Cut along the cutting line, taking care not to cut the inlay, and clip to the pins at both ends.

Remove the tape from the side of the inlay that you're going to sew. Fold the seam allowances to the back, with right sides together, and pin them. The fabric edges should line up. Sew on the marked seamline, as shown in the bottom right drawing on the facing page. Knot the threads at the end of the seam and iron the seam allowances open or away from the direction of your next seam; if the seam allowances are ironed away from the next seam they won't get in the way when sewing.

Curved inlays are trickier to prepare. To help match the seams for sewing, I mark perpendicular to the penciled seam line on the background fabric every two inches and make corresponding marks on the inlay, as shown in the photo at lower right. Before I stitch the curved seam, I liberally clip the seam allowances so the two layers will lie flat.

Repeat the process for every side and piece that you'd like to inlay. Practice makes perfect; good luck.   □

Oppenheimer is a quilt artist and neon-sign designer in Oakland, CA. Her quilts have been included in four of the Quilt National exhibits.

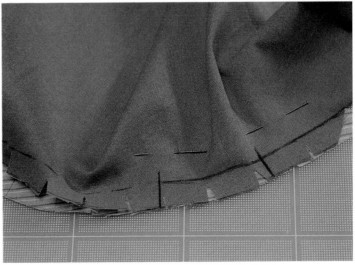

By laying a quilt-in-progress out on her table, Oppenheimer can trace many inlay patterns at once. Her studio includes a light table, a dyeing station, and a display wall.

Machine inlaying can be applied to curved pieces. Before you stitch a curve, mark the seams so they can be matched up, and clip seam allowances liberally, as Oppenheimer has done for the inlay at right.

Of Fractals, and Pixels, and Rotating Quilt Blocks

Using the computer as a quilt-design tool

by Lynne Heller

Lynne Heller runs a paint program on her color television using an Atari 520 ST computer. She controls the arrangement of lines by moving the "mouse" with her right hand. Each movement is mirrored in four quadrants of the screen to create a quiltlike pattern.

i often find myself sitting alone in front of my computer, late at night, talking to the machine. I've cajoled it, criticized it, congratulated it—you name it. And if it's really late at night, I've even imagined that it has answered back.

After I caught myself regularly trying to communicate with this hunk of inanimate plastic and metal, I started thinking about why. Perhaps it's because the machine is so much more than just a drafting tool—it's like an endless library of images and designs, and it generates new ones at my command. In fact, it's full of ideas for the taking. In my experience, the computer's capabilities can actually inspire artwork.

I'll be describing some of the ways I've used the computer's image-making potential to help me create quilt designs. Generally I use simple, accessible equipment, but I sometimes use more expensive rented equipment. Programs are available (or are being developed) that do everything I describe below on the least-expensive machines.

Paint programs

When I first heard about quilt design programs for the computer I was determined to get one. These programs are specifically used for the design of quilt blocks, traditional and otherwise. You can invent endless block variations or select from the built-in library of traditional blocks and borders. You can make multiple blocks and flip or rotate them until you find a block setting you like; then you can print out your design. A good example of these programs is PC Quilt, $35 postpaid from Nina Antze, 7061 Lynch Road, Sebastopol, CA 95472 (707-823-8494).

From *Threads* magazine (June 1990) 29:54-57

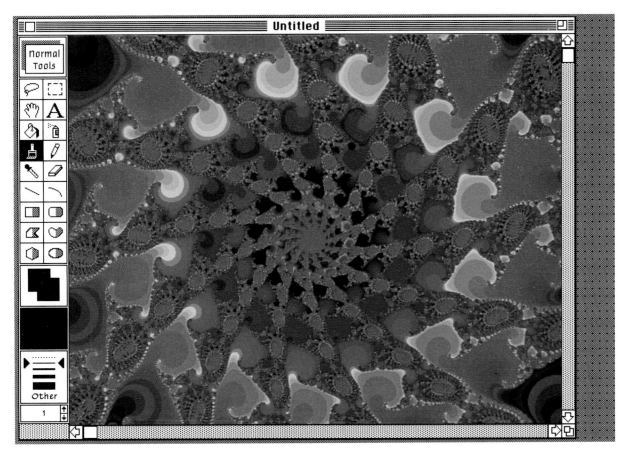

Untitled

Normal Tools

Other
1

This simulated screen from a Macintosh paint program shows a selection of symbols at left, called icons, which depict computer functions that emulate their real-world counterparts. The selected icon, a paint brush, indicates that the operator can change the colors in the design, choosing from the paint program's vast pallette. The image in the working area of the screen is part of a fractal design, derived from a formula that the computer ran automatically. Any part of this type of fractal can be continuously enlarged and new levels of detail will emerge, ad infinitum. (Photo by C. Partridge and L. Titze)

At first the quilt design programs I could find were all written for the IBM PC. I have an inexpensive Atari 520 ST (it plugs into my color television, and I've seen this model on sale for under $400), so I couldn't use those programs on my machine. It's now possible to run many IBM programs on the Atari (with a widely-available program called pc-ditto), but I was able to get an Atari paint program with many of the same capabilities (I bought Degas Elite, a popular paint program, for under $50).

In fact, quilt programs are basically specialized versions of paint programs, with a few added features that designers hope quilters will find useful. I'm interested in nontraditional quilts, so in some ways a paint program is more appropriate for me because it doesn't assume anything about what I want to make with it. I can design with or without blocks equally well on either program, but I might have to go through a few more steps to get my paint program to do things that the quilt program can do automatically—for example, creating geometric shapes that are common in traditional quilt blocks.

When you first look at a paint program's screen, you see a large empty area for creating your design, with images on the left (called icons, shown in the photo above) that offer choices about how you can make marks in the design area. With many computers you get a mouse—a

hand-held gadget that you can slide around on your work surface, as I'm doing in the photo on the facing page. As you move the mouse, marks appear in the design area; the kind of mark depends on the option you've selected. Many icons are images of familiar tools that function on the screen like their real-life counterparts. If you select a pencil icon, for example, when you move the mouse, you'll see a single-line mark move across the screen in the same direction. You can erase the marks you draw by choosing the eraser icon. You can airbrush, stipple, and paint, both with patterns and with solid colors.

If the jargon associated with computer programs puts you off, don't worry. The whole point of icons is to keep the process visual and intuitive, and it works; paint programs are a breeze to use. You choose your icon, click a button on the mouse, and draw away.

When I started playing with the different options in the paint program, I quickly came up with wonderful ideas for quilts that broke away from traditional block structure. I found the layering feature most intriguing. I could add layers of visual effects and patterns over my initial design, so that as I erased part of one layer, I'd reveal the layer underneath. The layers could even be transparent, which produced amazing depth and richness. Thus the paint program led me to

another way of working with the quilt structure. Now I think much more in terms of layers than of blocks.

More paint program features

Professional computer artists often have more than one paint program so that they can use the best features of each. Quite a few of these features lend themselves to quilt designing. Here are a few things a typical paint program can do.

The name paint program implies color, and this feature can be a revelation to quilt artists. Different computers and monitors have different color ranges, but even my Atari can show over 500 different colors when plugged into a color television. Most paint programs allow you to easily change the colors in your design in a matter of seconds.

When you're drawing lines, you can draw freehand, or choose straight lines, automatic circles, ellipses, squares, outlines with rounded corners, and polygons. Symmetrical designs are easy because you can choose to have any line or design you draw on half or a quarter of the screen appear mirrored in each of the other sectors.

The block option allows you to define any part of a drawing or design and repeat it anywhere else in the picture. You can stretch, distort, rotate, flip, or recolor the part any way you like, and the part can be any shape.

To simulate the look of pieces of fabric, enclosed shapes in a design have to be filled completely with solid colors or patterns. The "fill" feature allows you to quickly fill up areas of your design. You specify a color and a pattern, and then start indicating areas you want filled with it. The "outline" feature works in reverse: You splash down a color with a brush, and then you clarify this shape by enclosing it within an adjustable outline.

Drawing patterns by hand is time consuming; with a paint program, it's just a matter of clicking the correct buttons and seconds later you have a customized pattern in the area you want filled. The program I use comes with 32 stored patterns and makes it easy to create your own.

The computer screen is made of hundreds of tiny rectangles called pixels. The computer creates images by coloring each pixel, in the same way that images are created with dots of color in a pointillist painting. You can play with the apparent size of these pixels with the zoom option, which allows you to zoom in and enlarge the pixels on the screen. You can then change the color of each pixel individually.

When you select the mosaic or pixelization option for your design, the computer takes the number of pixels that you've specified—for example, a five-pixel by five-pixel area—and averages the color of these 25 pixels so they become one block of color. Then this averaging is done for the whole screen. The result is a geometric, boxy rendition of the original picture, like the screen images at right. The clarity of the original is reduced and the image is distorted and softened, but because it is always rendered in solid-color rectangles, it is very easy to translate this image from the screen into a usable quilt design.

Designs by formula

Paint programs turn the computer into a sort of automated sketch pad for you to draw on. But you can also have the computer do the designing and drawing by itself. When you see that it's done something you like, you can send the design over to your paint program for refinement.

Advanced paint programs can generate their own drawings with a technique called tweening, shown in the drawing above. You draw two different outlined shapes, select a few points on each outline, and tell the computer to transform one shape into the other, using your points as references and showing you as many steps along the way as you want. You can select a single step whose shape you like or you can use the entire progression in your final design.

Computers can also generate designs by running mathematical formulas that de-termine how to color each pixel on the screen. With the right software, you don't have to know the formulas; you just plug in a few variables, or tell the computer a range to pick from, and let it go. I've found several types of computer-generated designs to be marvelous for sparking off quilt ideas. The most dramatic examples are clearly the designs called fractals.

Fractals—Quilters have always used a very simple form of the fractal idea in their work. Imagine a square quilt divided into square blocks. Each of these blocks is a fourpatch made up of four squares. Each

see the same pattern twice, but all the parts are similar, like the image on p. 81 (called iterated fractals); and those in which a single shape is repeated, but made smaller, like the squares in the example above (called recursive fractals).

Once you have plotted an iterated fractal on your screen, you can zoom in on any section and the computer will recalculate the points of this selected section. Instead of seeing just an enlargement of what you saw previously, as you would with a recursive fractal, you'll see whole new formations based on the original shape. You can go zooming in on the same

Tweening

Given two solid shapes, the computer transforms one shape into the other, showing several steps along the way; above are two different paths connecting the same shapes.

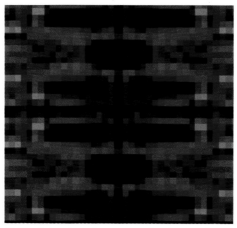

Heller "mosaic-ed" a computer image by averaging the colors into small squares; then she zoomed in and averaged again to create a new image. (Photo by Christine Partridge and Les Titze)

square is further divided into four squares. The smallest unit has the same shape as the largest unit, the overall quilt. This is called self-similarity, and it's part of the fascination of fractals. You can look at computer-generated fractals forever and always see new levels of similarity between the overall and the detail.

Simple programs that generate fractal designs exist for all computers. I've used a public-domain program for the Atari called Fractal Factory, as well as programs for the Macintosh. With them I've explored two kinds of fractals: those in which you never

section forever, so each iterated fractal you generate is a source of an infinite number of unique designs.

Handmade fractals—Another group of fractals is randomly generated. The basic principle is simple enough that you can create them without a computer, and my design at lower left on p. 83 is an example.

The technique starts with a selected geometric shape. If you're doing it by hand, it's easiest to use a triangle; I drew a large one on a piece of tracing paper. I located the midpoints of all three sides and then

cardboard sewing board printed with a 1-in. grid, sold in most home sewing stores. Lay the board underneath your quilt top; the grid will be visible through light-colored fabrics. If your layout includes a series of borders, use the gridded sewing board to measure and mark off preliminary guidelines first.

Then position the paper patterns underneath the fabric, and trace the stitching lines of the major motifs. Reposition the patterns as needed to mark each section.

The challenge of marking is to make lines that will show during the lengthy quilting process, but will be undetectable once the quilting is done. Many old whitework quilts show no evidence of either marks or laundering. Either the fabric was so lightly marked that the quilting thread covered the pattern lines or the tops were "needle marked." To needle mark, the quiltmaker traced with a dull yarn needle

Sources

The Cotton Patch
1025 Brown Avenue
Lafayette, CA 94549
(415) 284-1177
Fabric (including wide muslin), notions, books, Orvus paste. Catalog $3.

Great American Quilt Factory, Inc.
8970 E. Hampden Avenue
Denver, CO 80231
(303) 740-6206
Books, patterns, notions, Orvus paste. Catalog $2.

Kalona Kountry Kreations
Sara Miller
RR 1
Kalona, IA 52247
(319) 656-5366
Fabric (including wide muslin and lightweight wool challis), notions, Orvus paste, some patterns.

Further Reading

Brackman, Barbara. *Clues in the Calico, A Guide to Identifying and Dating Antique Quilts.* McLean, Virginia: EPM, 1989.

Colby, Averil. *Quilting.* New York: Charles Scribner's Sons, 1971.

Cory, Pepper. *Quilting Designs from Amish Quilts.* Martinez, California: C & T Publishing, 1985.

Fons, Marianne. *Fine Feathers.* Martinez, California: C & T Publishing, 1988.

Orlofsky, Patsy, and Myron Orlofsky. *Quilts in America.* New York: McGraw-Hill, 1974.

Oshins, Lisa Turner. *Quilt Collections, A Directory for the United States and Canada.* Washington: Acropolis Books, Ltd., 1987.

Osler, Dorothy. *Traditional British Quilts.* London: B.T. Batsford Ltd., 1987.

Safford, Carlton L., and Robert Bishop. *America's Quilts and Coverlets.* New York: E.P. Dutton, 1980.

or rug needle held at an oblique angle, pressing the quilting line into the fabric. Quilting had to be done before the faint groove made by the needle relaxed. The practitioners of this technique deserved a prize not only for their quilting skills, but for their eyesight!

Marking tools—Various marking tools have been in and out of favor with quilters over the decades. Old-time markers included cinnamon, chalk, and soap. The felt-tip chemical marker whose blue ink disappears with washing or the application of water, eagerly embraced by quilters in the late 1970s, is no longer recommended, except possibly for works that will receive regular washings, such as garments. Residue from the ink has sometimes reappeared years later, turning the fabric brown and even rotting it.

The best tool for marking designs on light- or medium-colored fabrics is a pencil that can hold a fine point so your lines will be thin. A mechanical pencil works well because it doesn't have to be sharpened. Use size 0.5 hard (H) leads. Another good marker is an artists' type silver pencil, such as Berol Verithin, sharpened frequently during marking. A new washable graphite pencil much applauded by those who have tried it is Berol Karisma Graphite Aquarelle.

Mark quilting lines just darkly enough so you can see them for quilting. If you make a mistake, a thin, lightly marked line may hardly show or you may be able to rub it off. I have had good luck washing out silver pencil lines after quilting. Some quilt shops sell erasers such as Faber-Castell's vinyl "Magic-rub" to use on mismarked lines. Don't rub the fabric too hard or you'll mar the surface.

After marking the primary motifs, mark the background grids or lines. Position the gridded sewing board under the fabric top so that the gridlines run in the direction you want the background stitching. Align a ruler with the printed lines to maintain true right angles. Reposition the board as needed to connect gridlines.

Marking dark fabrics—Marking elaborate quilting on darker fabrics through which you can't see the lines of your pattern is especially challenging. For a small project you can use a light table setup, such as a glass-topped coffee table with a light underneath it, for tracing the pattern lines. Or tape the fabric and pattern to a glass door or window and use sunlight to backlight your pattern. For full-size quilts, however, this approach is not feasible.

After working out your designs on paper, make templates for each motif. Thin, opaque plastic designed especially for

quiltmakers works well. Lay pieces of the plastic on your paper patterns and trace the outlines. Cut out the templates with scissors, making the curves as smooth as possible. Mark the fabric by drawing around the templates with silver or white artists' pencils, repositioning the templates as needed. When using templates, often you can mark only the outlines of designs. Fill in the inner lines by eye later. The drawing on the facing page shows what templates for my quilt look like.

Putting it all together

Layer the backing, the batting, and the marked quilt top. Thread baste the layers together, working from the center outward and basting 4 in. to 6 in. apart both horizontally and vertically. For this task, it's best to lay the quilt out flat on several tables pushed together, even if this means taking your work elsewhere.

Many brands of batting are available, some of them all-cotton, some synthetic, and some blends. Most quilters choose a low-loft batt for a whole-cloth quilt so the smallest stitches are possible.

You can quilt in a frame or with a hoop. Start at the center and work toward the outer edges. To bind the edges, I prefer self-fabric, bias binding. To make a durable binding, I cut a 2½-in. wide continuous binding (see the instructions on p. 43) and fold it in half. Don't trim away excess backing and batting until after you machine stitch the prepared bias to the edge of the quilt top. Mark a placement line on the quilt top ¼ in. outside the desired finished edge. Align the raw edge of the folded binding with the marked placement line. Stitch with a ¼-in. seam allowance. Don't trim the batting flush with raw edges of bindings; leave a little batting to fill the binding. Turn the folded edge and stitch it in place.

If you wish to wash your completed quilt to eliminate the marked lines (or because it's gotten dirty from so much handling), use cold water, the large-load setting on your machine, and a specialized detergent such as Orvus paste (see "Sources" at left).

An elaborate whole-cloth quilt takes hours, weeks, months, and maybe even years of quilting. No matter how well you quilt when you begin, your stitches will probably be even better when you're finished. As you spread your whole-cloth beauty on your best bed, you'll feel you've graduated from artisan- to master-class among quilters. □

Marianne Fons, a frequent contributor to Threads, *is the author of* Fine Feathers, *a book on customizing traditional feather quilting designs, and several other quilting books. She teaches nationally.*

Custom-made Feather Rings

Designing perfect plumes to fit any quilt

by Marianne Fons

*f*eather motifs in needlework have probably been around since the first warrior stuck an ostrich plume in his helmet to catch a lady's eye. As early as the 13th century, English monks used curling lines of feathers to decorate the margins of their illustrated parchments. Ornamental feathers became so popular by the 14th century that the Black Prince (Prince of Wales and eldest son of Edward III) adopted a personal badge of three curled feathers. It remains the official insignia of the Prince of Wales today. Extant English quilted garments and bedding from the 17th century onward display elegant feather motifs.

Feather borders, wreaths, and fancies appear on historic quilts from every decade of American quiltmaking, and like any folk art, were modified and added to as they were shared by quilters from different communities. Some of the first quilts made by American colonists were whole-cloth coverlets without patchwork or appliqué, just intricate stitching through the top, filler, and backing. Many have rich feather motifs on the borders of their medallion-style designs. During the great flowering of American patchwork and appliqué in the 19th century, quilters everywhere used feather designs, especially rings, to enhance the bold and beautiful surfaces of their quilts.

Perhaps the most famous users of feather quilting designs were the Pennsylvania Amish, who, from 1870 to 1950, embellished bold geometric surfaces of "plain" wool with exquisite quilting. A large central star ringed by a circle of feathers and wide cloth borders filled with curving plumes, much like the quilt shown in the photo on the facing page, are trademarks of the best Amish quilts. No one knows why the Amish, who felt that the use of printed fabrics in quilts was too worldly, stitched the fanciest possible quilting designs.

Feather quilting designs are as popular today as ever. The gentle sweep of quilted plumes seems to enhance the graceful lines of appliqué and the hard edges of patchwork equally well. But despite the great wealth of new quilting books, templates, and tools, many quilters are still frustrated by feather designs. Because of all the curving lines of feather motifs, needleworkers often hesitate to redraw patterns to fit their own quilts. I used to think a person had to be born Amish to originate a feather ring!

Feather rings and scrolls abound on the strong geometric quilts made by the Pennsylvania Amish between 1870 and 1950 (left). To many quilt enthusiasts, fine feathering is virtually synonymous with Amish quilting. (Photo courtesy of The Esprit Quilt Collection)

Marianne Fons marks a feather ring (right) on dark fabric with a plastic template that she made. Having drawn the feathers of the outer ring, she completes the inner one.

Feather quilting designs, however, are not really hard to create. Undulating plumes that wind continuously around the border of a quilt, as well as feather circles, hearts, and other fancies, are easy to make from scratch once you learn feather basics.

Understanding feather motifs—All feather motifs are made up of individual scallops that are actually half-hearts lined up perpendicular to a center vein, which can be single or double to represent the hard quill of a feather. Each of these individual half-heart feather shapes begins with a full, rounded "hump" opposite the vein and ends with a "tail" that curves into the vein, ending just under the starting point of the hump. On one side of the vein, the feathers are right sides of hearts; on the other side, they're left sides (see the top-left drawing, page 90).

An interesting fact about feather quilting designs is that they are never perfect. In studying feather designs on Amish and other antique quilts, I've found that some imprecision actually contributes to the organic beauty of flowing feathers. The number of feathers along each section of a border doesn't have to be the same, nor must each scallop of a feather ring be identical. Feathers shouldn't look machine-produced.

Making a feather ring—You can put the following basics into practice to construct your own feather ring:
1. Determine the outer dimension of your circle. If, for example, you have a 10-in.-sq. area on your quilt that you want to fill with a feather circle, your circle should have a 9-in.-dia. (or smaller) to allow some air space between the quilting stitches and the outer boundary of the square, often a seam. Cut out a piece of paper the size of your square—in this example, 10 in. Fold

the square in half twice to find its center. Then use a compass to draw a 9-in.-dia. (4½-in. radius) circle on the paper. For larger circles, you may need to use household templates, such as pot and pan lids or bowls and plates. You can also create your own compass in any size with a tack and a piece of string.
2. Decide how wide you want the individual feathers to be. A width of 1½ in. works well for a 4½-in. radius. Draw a second circle inside the first one, this time with a 3-in. radius. This will be the center vein of the feather ring. If you want a double vein, draw a third circle, ¼ in. inside the first vein line. So that you can have feathers on each side of the center vein, draw one more circle 1½ in. inside the vein (see top-right drawing, page 90).
3. Use a coin to form guiding scallops along the inside of both outer guidelines. A quarter is a good size for a 9-in. ring. A big circle with perhaps a 30-in. dia. might require a quilting-thread spool as a guide. It is important when you draw around the coin to use almost the entire half (see bottom-left drawing, page 90). As you come scalloping around to the place where you began, you must fudge several scallops to come out even.
4. Once you've made these guiding scallops, you're ready to complete the half-heart shapes of the feathers. Draw right-hand sides of hearts on the outside of the center vein and left-hand sides of hearts on the inside. Notice that the feathers appear to flow in a clockwise direction (see bottom-right drawing, page 90). That's because right sides of hearts have been used in the outer ring. A counterclockwise ring would have left sides of hearts to the outside. Complete the outer ring first. Draw a smooth curve over the coin hump and down into the center vein just under the beginning of the hump. Always add half-hearts

in the direction that a feather plume is flowing. Keep the feather shapes plump and rounded, and bring the tails gently into the center vein so the line remains curved from beginning to end.

5. If the outer ring had right-hand sides of hearts, as it does here, draw left-hand sides on the inner ring. This ring has far fewer feathers than the outer one, but the amount of space at the center vein is virtually the same. Draw the feathers for the inner ring just as you did for the outer ring, with the tails ending up right under the starting point of the humps. The amount of space between the tails along the center vein will be greater, though, and the feathers

will appear to have elongated tails. Dotted lines on several individual feathers, as shown in the drawing at bottom right, reveal that each feather is still a simple half-heart.

6. When you're satisfied with the feather circle that you've drawn, use a permanent black marking pen to darken the lines so you can see them through fabric to mark quilting lines. If you want to put your circle on a dark fabric and mark from the top, you can make templates by tracing the finished circles onto thin opaque plastic and cutting them out. Trace around the edges, as shown in the photo on page 89.

Feather rings are much easier to make than it would appear. Now when you find a

picture of a feather motif that would be perfect for your quilt, use pencil, paper, and coins to adapt it to the size you need. And with experimentation, you can customize feathers for shapes such as hearts, squares, ovals, and irregular forms. You can also create undulating feather borders that wind around a quilt by forming repeats and placing them end to end. □

Marianne Fons enjoys designing quilts, writing about quilting, and teaching. Her most recent quilting book is Fine Feathers, C & T Publishing, Lafayette, CA, 1987; $15.50 (P&H included), available from Meadowlark Farm, RR 3, Box 95, Winterset, IA 50273.

Understanding the feather motif

Half-hearts are placed perpendicular to vein.

Constructing the feather ring

Find center of square by folding twice; then draw concentric circles. The width of the two feather rings should be the same.

Use a coin to scallop guidelines along edges furthest from vein.

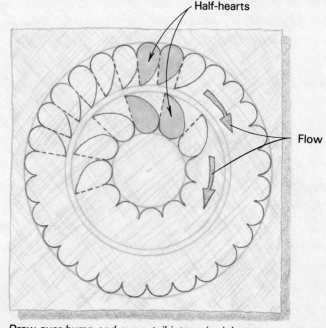

Draw over hump and curve tail into vein right below it.

Layered Trapunto

A technique for raised quilting that you can stretch and frame or spread on the bed

by Lois Morrison

i thought I had invented trapunto. I had been studying composition, working on Titian's "Venus and the Organ Player." I was fascinated by the three-dimensionality of his Venus. It was clear that "she-in-the-round" was what the painting was about. At that time I was making some stuffed toys for the children, and I thought, "If I pin a piece of cloth on the back of my painting, sew Venus's outline, and stuff her, I will have a real, three-dimensional painting." That's exactly what I did, and it worked; I held in my hands a plump little nude in a painting. Then I began leaving the painting part out.

I called these pieces "pattables" because people kept wanting to touch them. Eventually, someone used the word *trapunto* and explained it to me. As I got more involved, I discovered that although I had invented it for myself, trapunto had a long history. There are, for example, some wonderful Sicilian pieces dating from about 1400, such as the one shown in detail at right, depicting the story of Tristan. Trapunto has been used on petticoats, caps, robes, quilts, and anything that quilting might also decorate. For more background, see *Trapunto and Other Forms of Raised Quilting,* by Mary Morgan and Dee Mosteller (Charles Scribner's Sons, 1981).

Basic trapunto—*Stuffed work,* an Early American term; *trapunto,* from the Italian *trapungere,* meaning to embroider; *white-on-white,* the most elegant of quilts—they all use the same technique. Two pieces of fabric are pinned or basted together, the outlines of the parts to be raised are sewn, and only those areas are stuffed. A traditional stuffing method is to use a loosely woven cloth for the back layer, to tease apart the threads of the fabric with a needle so stuffing can be poked into the desired areas, and then to tease the threads back in place.

I prefer to use a whole piece of cloth for the front and to sew bits of backing cloth only in the areas I want to stuff. If I'm making a quilt for a bed, I finish off by sewing another whole piece of cloth, right sides together, along three edges. I then turn the quilt right side out and finish the fourth edge. But usually I stretch and frame my pieces to hang on the wall. The stretching removes background wrinkles and makes the relief slightly lower.

Whether or not I plan to stretch the piece, this is how I proceed. I have on hand off-white or white fabric, like unbleached or bleached muslin, a needle and thread, washable loose stuffing (polyester is fine), pencil and paper, pins, and a slender knitting needle for pushing in the stuffing. I take a simple shape, like that of my dog (see bottom photos at right), and draw its outline on paper. I cut that out and use it as a stencil, drawing around it on the cloth. I place a second piece of fabric that's a bit larger than the outline behind the first and pin it in place. On the front of the piece I sew along the outline, using a backstitch, which locks in place. Its size and tension are easy to control. (A running stitch or machine stitch will also work.) I leave a small opening along the outline as I sew, stuff the area, and finish the seam later. Sometimes I stitch around the whole shape, turn the work over, and slit the back just enough so that I can push in the stuffing. Then I whipstitch the slit shut. Some people use a hoop when stitching, but I don't find it necessary.

How much to stuff is a matter of preference. Because two of the dog's legs and an ear are in the background, I stuffed these areas more lightly than the rest of the dog so they would appear to recede. The more stuffing, the higher the relief and the more puckering or waving of the fabric around the edge. The decision rests on how much waving you can accept versus the firmness you want. You can pack in more stuffing if you plan to stretch the piece.

Layered trapunto—When using the basic technique, I had a problem doing human figures, as all of the parts looked embedded. The nose and the breasts—any part that should protrude—sank awkwardly back into the body. An overlap, like an arm crossing the body, was a disaster. It took me a while, but I finally worked out a layering technique that produces a true bas-relief.

I begin with a drawing. For the piece illustrated on page 101, I had a drawing I liked and a Xerox of a foot skeleton from *Gray's Anatomy.* Because the piece is relatively small (17 in. by 16 in.), I chose unbleached muslin. Had it been larger, I would have used unbleached cotton canvas.

A word about materials. I use those two fabrics exclusively. For small works, the muslin takes the details best, but for larger pieces, cotton canvas takes the stress of stretching better. Pure-white fabric is too harsh, but any colored or dark fabric, such as natural linen, causes the work to disappear into the background. For my wall pieces, kapok is the only stuffing for me. This silky fiber (from the seed pod of the tropical ceiba tree) is not washable—it will bleed through and stain the surface if it gets wet—but wool and synthetic stuffings have too much life in them. They bounce back out of nooks and crannies. Cotton is too dead—it lumps up quickly. Kapok slips into its spot and stays there—it doesn't lump. I like a cotton thread, preferably quilting weight so that it tangles less.

At this point I iron the fabric and do a careful tracing of the drawing to use as a stencil. I cut out the whole figure, lay it on the fabric, and draw around it. Then I transfer the interior lines to the fabric by cutting each drawn line of the stencil and penciling along the cut edge. The tissue-paper stencil is in shreds by the time I am through, but the drawing is on the fabric.

I must now decide what in the drawing is closest to me; that is, what should be sewn and stuffed first. As each subsequent layer is sewn and stuffed, it pushes the layer beneath it further forward. To begin, I pin bits of fabric behind the foreground areas, and using a small backstitch, I begin sewing on the front of the fabric, along the pencil lines, leaving a knot on the back. I also knot the thread tail on the back when I finish. If the area is to blend into another area (as the top of the knee does to the upper leg, for example) I do not sew it completely, but pin it shut from the front so

Trapunto, or raised quilting, gives life and depth to this 15th-century Sicilian hanging, which tells the story of Tristan. The double-layer linen cloth is stitched with brown and natural linen thread and stuffed with cotton. Photo courtesy of the Victoria and Albert Museum, London.

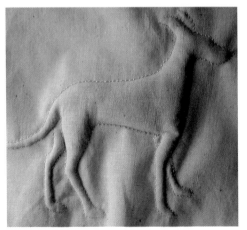 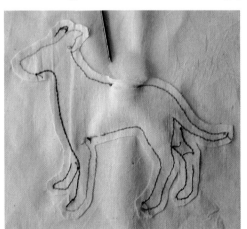 

To make a simple raised form like this dog, Lois Morrison pins a backing piece to the cloth and stitches along her traced lines. She usually leaves a portion of the line unsewn, stuffs in kapok or polyester, and completes the stitching. Sometimes, as at right, she slits the backing of the fully-stitched area, then stuffs it and stitches the slit closed with an overcast stitch. At left, the completed dog in relief.

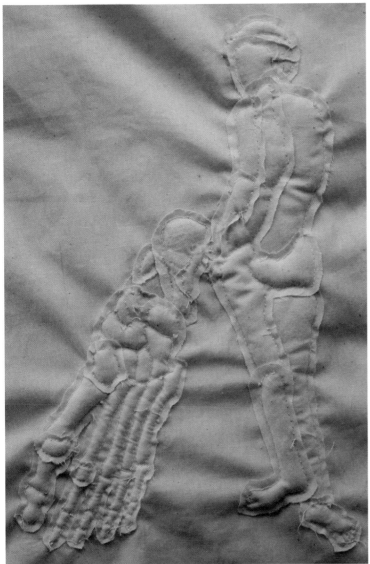

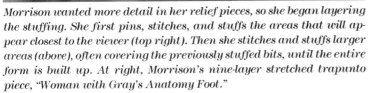

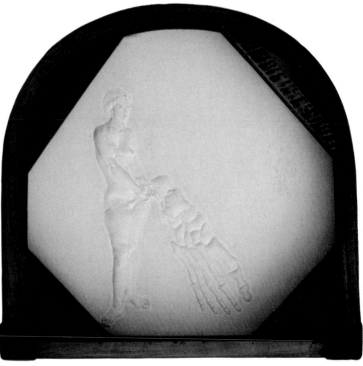

Morrison wanted more detail in her relief pieces, so she began layering the stuffing. She first pins, stitches, and stuffs the areas that will appear closest to the viewer (top right). Then she stitches and stuffs larger areas (above), often covering the previously stuffed bits, until the entire form is built up. At right, Morrison's nine-layer stretched trapunto piece, "Woman with Gray's Anatomy Foot."

the stuffing won't shift about. This pin must remain until the figure is stretched in the frame. Turning the fabric over, I push the kapok into the sewn area, using a knitting needle. For a truly small space, I use the eye of the embroidery needle. For an area that is completely outlined, I leave just a bit of the stitching line open to get the stuffing in. Then I continue sewing to close it off. I trim any extra fabric to about ¼ in. from the stitching.

I sew and stuff the second layer the same way. When one layer partially overlaps another, I stitch along the pencil line until I reach the end. I bring the needle to the back, turn the piece over, and continue sewing about ¼ in. through only the layer closest to me on the back. This attaches the layers invisibly, creating a subtle continuation of the sewn line, as at the figure's hairline in the photo at bottom right, above. I constantly finger the piece as I stuff. Gauging how tightly to stuff is a matter of experience. After you've sewn

and stuffed a section, you can make a small slit, add or remove stuffing, and sew it up again with an overstitch—even after you've stretched it.

Once all the sewing, stuffing, pinning, and trimming are done, I position the piece in its frame and tape it there. I turn it over and begin stretching it from the back. I use carpet tacks and, with a tack hammer, I put one tack in the middle of each side. I don't drive the tacks in all the way until every tack is in place and I've turned the piece over to ensure that it is exactly the way it should be. Next, I place tacks on both sides of the four tacks and continue to stretch and tack, moving toward the corners. After a final check, I drive the tacks in with a regular hammer. I trim the fabric a bit wider than the frame and tack the edges down, using just enough tacks to secure it.

Then I turn the piece over, remove the pins, and with my fingers and a needle, smooth out the pinholes. Like a raised tent,

the piece has come alive. The lumpy mess full of pins is now taut and smooth, the forms standing out clearly from the fabric.

If stretching is not for you, keep the stuffing looser. A stretched piece is crisp in feeling, whereas an unstretched piece is more flexible. And if you want to work with color, be careful—it may obscure the good work you have done. If you wish to add color by appliquéing, stitching, dyeing, or staining, do it before you begin sewing the trapunto. You can paint with opaque colors after you stretch the sewn piece, but be sure to mask the edges of your frame.

Trapunto can be used in a number of ways. It can be as simple as stuffing the flowers or horses on an already-printed piece of fabric or as complex as a multilayered bas-relief. It can grace a child's garment, a baby's cap, a warm petticoat, a white quilt, or a wall hanging. □

Lois Morrison lives in Leonia, NJ. All photos by the author, except where noted.

Quilt Notebook

Tips

Making perfect borders for rugs and quilts

Many of my students of traditional rug hooking had trouble figuring out a repeat-pattern border design because the math can be tricky. But this method makes the task very simple and remarkably effective. Although the border treatments for the long and short sides won't be exactly the same, they can be made to come out pretty close, and they'll save you lots of time and frustration. The method also works well for figuring out quilt borders.

1. Decide how deep you want the border to be, and mark off this area (drawing at left, below).

2. Cut a strip of newspaper or freezer paper the length and width of the longer borders of your rug, omitting the corner squares.

3. Fold the strip evenly as many times as you want to accommodate the repeat (drawing at right, below). Trace the repeat on one folded section, and transfer it to the burlap. If you're doing something simple, like a scalloped edge, cut the scallop from the accordion-folded paper, unfold it, and trace the pattern directly onto the rug.

4. Repeat steps 2 and 3 for the shorter sides of the rug.

5. Choose an appropriate corner motif and add it to each corner.

–Jean Baker White, North Haven, ME

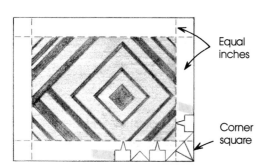

Mark off rug's border area from edge to edge on all four sides.

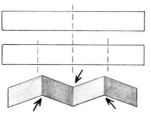

Fold strip evenly to accommodate repeat.

Draw design and transfer.

Illustration by Bob LaPointe

Perfect hexagons for quilters

This shortcut for quilters working with hexagons uses the paper-lining technique (drawings below). As paper liners I use the return postcards inserted in magazines. The obvious advantages are that you need only six stitches per patch, and you leave them in the work after removing the paper. The patches have stable, crisp edges and are easy to whipstitch together.

This method works well on all fabrics, particularly delicate ones, where basting stitches might leave marks on the right side of the work when the patch is pressed, as in the sew-through-the-paper system. Also, when whipping the prepared hexagons to each other, you needn't worry about your needle picking up the paper edge, as there's no paper. The postcards are free and heavy enough to be used many times.

–Mary Alice Hanson, Seattle, WA

Cut hexagonal patches from fabric, with seam allowances; and cut paper pattern without seam allowances. Pin pattern on wrong side of fabric, using two pins to maintain straight grain.

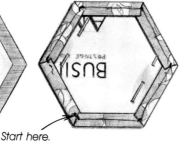

Start here.

Fold seam allowance over paper edges, one edge at a time. Take one backstitch at each of six corners. Don't sew through paper.

Remove pins, leave paper in, and press patch on both sides. Then remove paper, but retain stitches.

Punch and Poke: Quilting Without Thimbles

by Sandra Millett

Several years ago I was sitting at a quilt show demonstrating my quilt-as-you-go technique, when I suddenly found myself surrounded by 40 gaping quilt lovers and one irate, opinionated quilter. I was quilting all wrong, and she couldn't stand it.

I had fallen in love with quiltmaking in 1975. It combines all the things that I enjoy—color and design, the technical aspects of drafting and precise execution, plus the touch of fabrics.

My biggest problem was trying to cope with the running stitch. I had read everything I could find on quilting, but information on how to actually do it was generally scarce: "Quilt it with white thread and tiny running stitches." I could figure out how to do the running stitch, but I couldn't seem to avoid puncturing the end of my right middle finger, with blood spots turning all fabrics into pin-dot prints.

I know you are wondering why I just didn't use a thimble. My mother and grandmother tried valiantly to convince me that one could not possibly sew properly without one. My fingers did not agree, however, and refused to work if a thimble was even in the room. I've since learned that other stitchers feel the same—half of my students abhor the darn thing.

Thimbles, tape, and finger holes were not my only problems. I couldn't take a large enough bite of the quilt backing. Sometimes the needle missed entirely. And I couldn't always supply enough pressure to push the needle through all the quilt layers. I concluded that the running stitch was not for me. What then would I do?

It seemed most logical that one hand should stay on top to punch the needle down and the other hand should remain below the work to receive the needle, turn it around, and poke it back up to the surface: The punch-and-poke stitch was born.

I soon found that it was not as easy as I had imagined. The stitches and spaces on the quilt top looked even and straight right from the start, but on the underside the needle was coming up all over the place, and usually nowhere near the quilting line.

frames to concentrate or circumscribe the energies generated inside the quilts. After she has attached the layers, Busch hand-bastes the entire pieced surface to batting and back.

The final step is the hand quilting, or stitching, done on a hoop. For Busch, this stitching is not merely a method of securing the quilt sandwich, but an enhancement of texture. "Quilting stitches border on sculpture," she says. "The direction of the quilting lines is just as important as the rest. Take that quality away, and the quilt would have a completely different kind of feel." In earlier work, the stitches form loop and arch patterns that take on a life of their own, working their spirited way over and around the hard edges of the color blocks. In recent work, the quilting stitches tend to form geometric grids. They offer the only element of order in "America est Patria Nostra." In "Maine Coast Video," some of the overquilting is done with long stitches of yarn; beads sewn at intervals recall the traditional tying and knotting method of holding the quilt together.

Busch's anomalous quilts inevitably raise the steamy fine art-versus-crafts question. That issue, she says, doesn't mean much to her. "I come from a painting background, and I'm just adding another process. Anyway, I find I'm in hot water with both camps." A quilt jury recently ruled that "Dorothy" didn't fulfill the standards of a quilt. On the other hand, art purists might object to Busch's reliance on the quilt-sandwich structure to achieve her aesthetic ends. Arguably, with an abstract painting as the basis of each of her quilts, Busch belongs—however unsteadily—in the fine-arts camp, and how well she fares should depend on an entirely different (and ultimately far more stringent) set of rules than any the craft camp can impose.

In fact, Busch is one of a small coterie founding a middle camp between crafts and art. Her quilts are useful signposts in the saga of applied arts moving into the insistently nonfunctional realm. Her works reveal the artist having a go at the quilt form—taking it apart and bringing insights to that tradition-bound medium. □

Linda Dyett, of New York City, is a contributing editor of Threads *magazine. Elizabeth Busch is director of Maine's "Percent for Art Program," which provides funds for the acquisition of art works for public buildings. Photos by Elizabeth Busch.*

In "Whispers," 1983 (top right), Busch includes all of the components of a traditional quilt sandwich, except for a finishing bias tape. Instead, she displays the structure, allowing the edges of the batting and the cloth to contribute to the overall texture. At right, a painted canvas sky is scored by machine stitching and strewn with appliquéd squares and triangles—domesticity gone amok in "Dorothy," 1984, from the Wizard of Oz *tryptych.*

Sunprints can be made by laying real objects or photographic negatives on treated fabric and exposing the setup to the sun. For "Pipes" Carol Adleman let the sun shine through negative and positive photograph images of PVC pipe and chain link fence onto red and yellow fabric. (53½ in. X 62 in.; 1985; photo by Christine Benkert)

Sunprinting for Quiltmakers

Catch the sun to create unique fabrics

by Carol Adleman

One look out the window tells me whether or not it is a day to work. "Catching the light"—specifically the sunlight—is essential for blueprinting on the fabrics I use for my wall quilts.

Printing my own fabric gives me an extra measure of control over my work and adds a dimension that purchased fabric cannot. Blueprinting is a way to create unique fabrics for just about anything—pieced or appliquéd quilts, fabric collages, wearable art. And don't forget the borders and bindings of quilts or linings of garments.

Blueprinting is a direct process similar to the printing of a black and white photograph. You saturate fabric with a solution of ferric salt, let the fabric dry, and then expose it to ultraviolet light, which turns the fabric blue. Areas that the light does not hit, because of folds in the fabric or objects that are placed on it, remain the color of the fabric. Rinsing in clear water washes away excess chemicals; the permanent image remains. The procedure for blueprinting on fabric is explained on p. 114.

Also referred to as cyanotype or sunprinting, blueprinting dates to about 1840 when it was invented by Sir John Herschel for producing architectural and mechanical drawings. Historically it has also been used to make botanical prints and for blueprinting one's own photos on postcards or on household items such as pillow covers.

Though the image produced is always blue, the shade and intensity vary; the blue can range from a turquoise to a navy. This restricted color palette poses a challenge to the artist to "push the blue" to its limit.

Manipulating the cloth

There are many ways to manipulate fabric so that light hits some areas but not others. Here are some suggestions.

Drape fabric over cones; place rings over the cones; drape fabric over cut-out shapes or small boxes. Indent fabric into Styrofoam cups. Wrap fabric around objects such as a ball, a marble, or a tube. Pleat fabric, into either stitched pleats or open folded pleats.

Patterns can be made by manipulating fabric. The fabric for "Stripes" was folded before exposure. (32 in. sq.; 1988; photo by Christine Benkert)

Crush or wrinkle fabric to create subtle shadows. Gather fabric by stitching a line of basting threads and pulling to gather; remove the stitches after printing.

Most fabric manipulations should be done after the fabric has been treated with the chemical solution, but stitched pleats and gathering should be done beforehand to keep the fabric from being exposed to light unnecessarily.

Photograms are the result of laying an object on the treated fabric and then sunprinting. You can use flat objects, such as lace or leaves, or three-dimensional objects, such as cut and folded paper. Press and dry leaves and flowers before printing, as the moisture content in fresh ones may affect the print.

When printing with a flat piece such as lace, cover the lace and fabric with clear glass or acrylic to ensure close contact and therefore a sharp print. Handling a large sheet of glass can be dangerous. Use glass in a picture frame to protect your hands from sharp edges; or tape the edges of the glass. Clear plastic or acrylic is safer, but unless it is thick, it may warp temporarily from the heat of the sun.

You can also print photographic negatives. Start with a good quality, high contrast black and white photo. Have either a *line negative* or a *halftone negative* made by a graphics printer. A line negative is all black and white with no gradations of gray, unlike a regular photographic negative. A halftone negative, which consists of many dots, creates the impression of grays. Halftone negatives can be made in various line screens. A 133-line screen usually works well. (For more on blueprinting photographs, see "From photographs to fabric" on the facing page.)

Since cyanotype is always somewhat experimental, I often blueprint a 12-in. or 15-in. square sample before proceeding with a large project to test the fabric as well as the negative or the method of fabric manipulation. To preview where the shadows will occur in a draped fabric piece or from a three-dimensional object, I arrange the untreated fabric and the objects as planned, then put the assemblage in the sunlight or under a lamp. Whatever is in shadow will remain the color of the cloth, although the angle of the sun during printing will affect the shapes of the shadows.

This method also gives you an idea of the quantity of fabric you'll need for a particular draping arrangement.

Light sources

The perfect day to print is a clear sunny day with no haze, low humidity, and little wind, but you can get good results with less than ideal conditions. If there is only partial sun, lengthen the exposure time, up to half an hour. Hazy sun seems to produce a more turquoise blue. If weather conditions change suddenly you can save the already treated but not yet exposed fabric for up to a week by storing the pieces in the dark.

I don't let the snow and cold of Minnesota stop me from printing year round. The most difficult aspect of working outdoors in the winter is clearing a spot in the snow to set the printing apparatus. Winter hours

for printing are pretty much limited to peak midday hours; I usually extend exposure time as well.

You can use a sun lamp as an indoor light source, but I have found that it requires a significantly longer exposure time (30 minutes minimum), and the image always seems to have a turquoise cast.

Fabrics

The more a fabric is able to absorb the chemicals, the darker the print will be. One hundred percent cottons are preferred but silk and linen can be used as well. Some silks seem to absorb better than others. I've had good luck with raw silk but less success with broadcloth; it's best to test the particular fabric. Unbleached muslins have been very satisfactory for me. Old linens and cottons in good condition are especially absor-

Basics of blueprinting on fabric

The chemicals needed to blueprint on fabric are *ferric ammonium citrate*, a yellow-green powder, and *potassium ferricyanide*, an orange-red powder; keep the powders in brown bottles or the light-resistant pouches they come in.

You can make up stock solutions of the two chemicals and store them for up to four months. Store them separately in brown bottles, and label and date the bottles. Once the two are mixed together, they remain potent for about two hours.

Wear rubber gloves and an apron or a smock when working with the chemicals in powder or liquid form, work in a well-ventilated area, and do not work in an eating area. Wear a

mask when working with the powdered chemicals and put newspaper on your work surface to collect any spilled powder; fold up and dispose of the newspaper. Keep chemicals away from children and pets.

Keep the equipment separate from kitchen utensils. Garage sale bowls and spoons work nicely.

For the first solution mix ⅓ cup (50 grams) of ferric ammonium citrate with 1 cup (250 ml.) water (preferably distilled) in a brown bottle, using a funnel. Cap the bottle and shake to dissolve the chemical. This solution tends to get moldy after about two weeks, but it is still usable; strain it as you pour to use it.

For the second solution add ⅛ cup (35 grams) of

potassium ferricyanide to 1 cup (250 ml.) water in another brown bottle. Shake to mix.

1. Mix equal amounts of the liquid solutions in a bowl just large enough to hold the saturated fabric. Start with ¼ cup of each; this will treat about 1 yd. of light- to medium-weight fabric.
Note: Work in low light from the time you mix the chemicals until you are ready to bring the fabric outdoors. I work in a windowless laundry room with only the light from an open door. You can also use a red or yellow light bulb.

2. Saturate the prewashed fabric in the mixture. Squeeze excess back into the bowl. Or apply the chemicals with a 1-in. paint brush. The fabric turns yellow-green when treated. I continue treating fabric until I've used up the solution.

3. Dry the treated fabric completely. You can iron it with a cool to warm iron to begin drying. Put three layers of newsprint above and below the fabric plus sheets of unprinted white paper next to the fabric if it's light colored. Then let the fabric air-dry flat in a darkroom or covered box. You can use a hair dryer to speed the drying. Always put layers of newsprint beneath wet or dripping fabric so as not to stain other surfaces.

4. On a flat, portable surface, layer the following items in order: fabric; the negative or other objects; and, if applicable, glass or acrylic. When printing anything three-dimensional or draped you do not need the glass.

Whenever possible drape the fabric and position all objects or negatives before carrying the piece outdoors. As soon as the sun hits the fabric the chemical reaction begins. A tabletop ironing board or a small bulletin board makes a good portable working surface; you can pin down small objects as well as the fabric itself. Or use a washout glue stick to hold the pieces in place.

5. Expose the assemblage in the sun for 5 to 30 minutes—5 to 10 minutes on a sunny summer day; 20 minutes on a sunny winter day. The fabric turns a gray-blue as it prints.

6. Rinse the fabric under running water until the water runs clear. In these small quantities the chemical solutions should not harm septic systems. You can darken the print by immersing the fabric for a few seconds in a solution of 1 quart water and 1 tsp. hydrogen peroxide (the 3% variety from the druggist). Rinse thoroughly in clear water and dry the fabric. —C.A.

Blueprinting fabric that's been draped over cones will create rough star-burst patterns. The fabric areas exposed to the sun turn a gray-blue; those hidden from light keep their original color. (Photo by Carol Adleman)

bent because they have been washed many times. Synthetic fibers won't absorb the chemicals, and only the natural fiber in a blend will absorb them. Try to avoid fabrics with finishes. Always wash and dry fabrics before applying the chemicals.

Fabrics that have a very fine weave with a high thread count will reproduce the most detail. This is important for printing a photographic negative. For a draped printing, a light- to medium-weight gauze-type fabric is good because it hangs with soft folds.

I like to use colored fabrics as well as white; bright colors work best. The color of the fabric naturally alters the shade of blue. Printing on yellow fabric produces a green shade; red fabrics yield a black tone.

Label or sort the fabrics in your collection as to which ones are especially good for blueprinting. Make notes of which brands work best. Test a fabric for its printability before embarking on a large project. Purchase a small quantity of silk, for example, before investing in yards of it.

Blueprinted fabric can be washed in a mild soap or dry cleaned. Do not use bleach or detergents containing phosphates. The print may fade if the fabric is left in the sun for a long time, but placing it in a dark room overnight will revive it. Blueprinted fabric is sensitive to alkaline, so don't store your works in acid-free tissue. ☐

Carol Adleman has been quilting for 20 years and blueprinting since 1980. She lives in the Minneapolis area, where she is active in quilt and surface design groups.

Supplies

Blueprint-Printables
1504 Industrial Way #7
Belmont, CA 94002
(800) 356-0445; in CA (415) 594-2995
Kits of pretreated fabric, T-shirts, etc. Catalog $2.

Donnelly Offset Negatives
269 Central Ave.
Rochester, NY 14605
(716) 232-3996
Kodalith negatives. Price list, send LSASE.

Gramma's Graphics, Inc.
20 Birling Gap, Dept. Thre-P1
Fairport, NY 14450
(716) 223-4309
Blueprinting kits and cotton fabrics. Catalog $1 and LSASE.

Photographers' Formulary, Inc.
PO Box 5105
Missoula, MT 59806
(800) 922-5255; in MT (800) 777-7158
Chemicals for blueprinting, bulk or kits. Catalog $1.

Testfabrics, Inc.
PO Box 420
Middlesex, NJ 08846
Natural fiber fabrics. Free catalog.

Photo by Tafi Brown

From photographs to fabric *by Tafi Brown*

To blueprint a photograph on fabric start with a sharp image free of extraneous background material. The photo should be simple and graphically strong. The most successful images are silhouettes; back-lit subjects; or simple subjects with either a lot of texture or very graphic shapes and lines, such as a white picket fence against the sky or a New England-style white clapboard house in early morning or late afternoon light. Fill the frame with your subject and keep the background as uncluttered as possible. Photograph people on a bright, sunny day when there are distinct shadows that will define the person's features.

The film and emulsion of common black-and-white negatives are too thin to block out enough sunlight to make a cyanotype print, so you must have a negative of your image made on graphic arts, or Kodalith, film. This high contrast film, which is used by graphic arts printers, has a thicker base and denser emulsion, thus blocking out all sunlight in the black areas and ensuring a good, clean white in the final cyanotype print.

You can often have Kodalith negatives made by a local graphics printer. They will normally work from a print, but some may be able to work from a slide. A color print or slide can be converted to black and white. Ask for a line negative made the exact size you want the blueprinted image to be. If the local printer can't make negatives, they or a graphic arts studio or photo studio may be able to refer you to someone who can. For Kodalith negatives by mail, see "Supplies" at left.

If you have a darkroom, you can make your own Kodalith negatives from slides, as I do, by putting the slide in the film carrier and the Kodalith film on the easel. You'll need a box of Kodalith film (about $100 for fifty 8 x 10 sheets) and graphic arts or lith developer.

To blueprint your negative on fabric, it's critical that you create a close contact between the fabric and the negative. A contact frame (available at photography supply stores) works well. You can also clamp the fabric and the negative between a pane of glass and a flat surface such as Masonite or another piece of glass.

Tafi Brown makes wall quilts incorporating cyanotype photographs.

Gilding the Lily
Embroidery stitches in Victorian crazy quilts

by Margaret Horton

Crusaders traipsing home from the Middle East in the 12th century were comforted by fancy new underwear. Thick quilted garments like those the Saracens borrowed from India or China must have made pleasant padding under the uncomfortable armor. During the 14th century in western Europe, similar padding provided warm bedcovers.

In America, such cozy quilts were especially needed, for the early settlers had no flocks of sheep to supply wool for blankets. Fabric was so scarce that women hoarded every scrap. They patched and repatched old quilts, and to avoid waste when making new ones, they pieced scraps together higgledy-piggledy. These early "crazy quilts" were definitely the poor relations of the usual bed furnishings, born of necessity and drab in appearance.

By the 19th century, American-made fabric was plentiful. Women didn't give up the tradition and sociability of quiltmaking, however, although the patterns became more formal. Then, in the last quarter of the 19th century, crazy patchwork was revived, not as a necessity, but so snippets of rich velvets, silks, and brocades from sumptuous garments could be used up and enjoyed. In addition to clothing scraps, fancy ribbons and even men's hatbands found their way into crazy quilts. Both of these have the advantage of not needing their edges turned under.

Vivid colors—the results of new dyes—also enlivened the pieced concoctions. These new colors satisfied the Victorian craving for novelty, but they were harsh and garish compared with the soft, natural dyes. Mauves, purples, and deep reds in particular appear in crazy quilts.

Not content with the richness of texture and color of the fabrics, Victorian ladies further embellished their patchwork with embroidery, frequently using gold-colored silk thread, so the quilts became as opulent as "scrambled eggs" on a naval uniform. Two types of embroidery were used. The larger patches often contain embroidered designs. Initials or monograms are often prominent, near the center of the quilts. Sometimes there are several, presumably of the various ladies who worked

Elaborate embroidery outlines the patches of this "Opera Singer's Crazy Quilt," ca. 1893. 67 in. by 70 in. Permanent collection of the Museum of American Folk Art; gift of Margaret Cavigga.

on the quilt or of family members. Among the countless other motifs are flowers, animals, and symbols of a special family interest, such as sports, music, or religion. Verses or short epigrams and prayers frequently appear on quilts. Although these cameos are often elaborate in design, the stitchery itself is usually simple, relying mainly on satin and outline stitches, giving the impression of needle painting. Large patches may also contain appliquéd figures secured with blanket stitches.

The second type of embroidery consists of decorative stitching along the joins of patches. It is this I find most interesting. Sometimes a single stitch (such as herring-

bone or feather) and color are used for the whole quilt, but often there are more. Although these edgings seem complex, they are usually worked with a few basic stitches, which zip along in no time. Herringbone, feather, and blanket stitches are the mainstays; outline, chain, and cross-stitches appear, as well as arrangements of straight stitches. The drawing on the facing page shows a variety of the stitches used.

The ingenuity involved in adapting simple stitches and concocting combinations is fascinating. There may be several lines of stitchery and many different-colored threads along each join. My mind boggled at the work in these crazy quilts until I realized that the

From *Threads* magazine (April 1987) 10:48-49

Embroidery stitches for crazy quilts

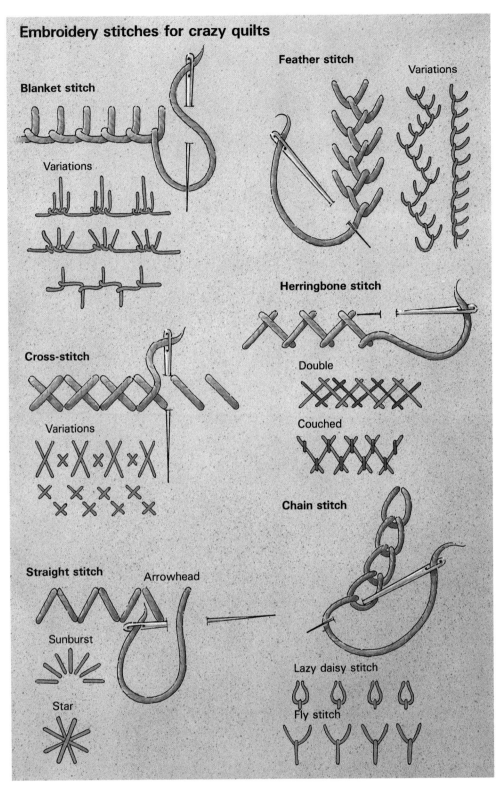

Blanket stitch

Variations

Feather stitch

Variations

Cross-stitch

Variations

Herringbone stitch

Double

Couched

Chain stitch

Lazy daisy stitch

Fly stitch

Straight stitch

Arrowhead

Sunburst

Star

Piecing a crazy quilt

The Victorians sometimes joined straight-edged pieces with simple running stitches. Stiff or thick fabrics and irregularly shaped patches were handsewn to a foundation of muslin or scrap fabric, their raw edges turned under as the work progressed. This method made assembly easier and helped prevent irregular or bias-cut pieces from stretching in use. Individual patches of delicate fabric were lined with batiste or another stabilizing fabric before assembly.

In the interest of economy, the oldest Victorian crazy quilts sometimes had newspaper foundations. The newspaper was usually torn away when the piecing was complete but sometimes was left to give the quilt extra body and warmth. Old letters provided a firmer foundation; one from the South contained some interesting reading from Confederate generals!

An alternate piecing method that's quick and easy to do by machine is to first baste a right-angled patch right side up to a corner of the foundation, as in the drawing below. Laundered, unbleached muslin provides a firm foundation. Place a second patch face down over the first and straight-stitch along the edge through both patches and the foundation. Turn the second patch right side up, and add others in the same way. Whether you do the piecing by hand or machine, you must turn under curved edges and any remaining raw edges before blindstitching, machine-topstitching, or embroidering them to the foundation. —*M.H.*

Machine piecing

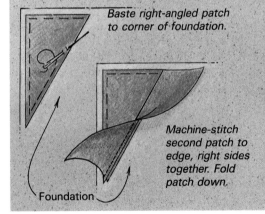

Baste right-angled patch to corner of foundation.

Machine-stitch second patch to edge, right sides together. Fold patch down.

Foundation

---

stitchery, although flamboyant, is not especially skillful or time-consuming.

Crazy quilts were sometimes assembled in one piece but more often were made in separate units—squares or rectangles of 12 in. to 18 in. These small units were easier to handle—more agreeable for working in the drawing room. The pieces were sometimes seamed together directly, producing interesting breaks in the crazy pattern, or joined in both directions with sashing strips, which are narrow strips of a single fabric. Plain, colored borders, usually of velvet, were often added.

Most of the decorative stitchery was done after the piecing of each unit was com-

plete, but sometimes fancy stitches served to sew down patches, particularly ribbons, hatbands, or other pieces with woven edges that did not need their edges turned under. The edges of bulky fabrics, like velvet, were sometimes left raw and covered by embroidery—often a closely worked blanket stitch.

Because of the many bulky seams and the greater weight of some of these rich velvets and brocades, crazy patchwork was not quilted but tied to its lining. Alternatively, the layers were secured by the seams joining separately made units. Mostly the work was not padded, so the pieces are really coverlets, not quilts.

Crazy quilts were very popular in their time. Manufacturers sold bundles of sumptuous scraps specifically for patchwork, some already painted or embroidered. These quilts are typically Victorian—rich and showy—yet simple to work. They were often smaller than bed-size and were used as show-off lap robes or throws. Queen Victoria had a crazy quilt draped over her piano. Supposedly everybody had one, yet an old Southern lady who once owned a crazy quilt told me, "It was a status symbol, for how many families could afford velvets and brocades?"□

Margaret Horton is a needlework designer, instructor, and lecturer in Atlanta, GA.

Drawing a Line with a Sewing Machine

Free-motion embroidery for creative quilting

by Damaris Jackson

My specialty is machine-embroidered quilting, which I do on both quilts and clothing, using my own line drawings as inspiration. This combination came about quite by chance ten years ago, when I started a series of pen-and-ink line drawings at the same time that I began an original quilt. Not surprisingly, much of the visual material for the quilt came from the line drawings.

I wanted to make the quilt my way, without outside influences, and I stubbornly hand-appliquéd corduroy animal silhouettes onto denim and hand-quilted through ½-in.-thick batting. That was my last hand-stitched quilt. As soon as I finished it, I turned to my 20-year-old Kenmore sewing machine to more efficiently test out the dozens of ideas it had stimulated.

Those early quilts were more like appliquéd comforters: animals and people floating in space and quilted on thick batting with a few additional vines and flowers to hold the back and front together. But my drawings went further than the big appliqué shapes, and I wondered how I could translate them into fabric. Using my sewing machine as a drawing tool was the answer.

Understanding line drawing—For my purposes, a line drawing is any single line that starts in one spot and then moves along, changing direction without breaks until a whole drawing (or section of a drawing) is done. It's like telling a story. You can use a writing implement or needle and thread, and one delightful aspect of the sewn drawings is that there are very few thread ends to knot, hide, or fray.

Line drawings can be designed as textures, doodles, or repeated patterns. In these modes they are particularly good for filling in space and differentiating one area from another when a different pattern is used in each.

Pictorial line drawings of objects or scenes are a little harder to draw, but they're more descriptive, more personal. They can be representational, as in realistic sketches or accurate and to-scale outlines of shapes. They can also be expressive, conveying a feeling or the idea of something through distortion or suggestion. I prefer to use the expressive type because it's the most interesting as an artistic statement.

A line, by definition, has motion. It is a point moving on a plane. It can go anywhere, do anything. A line, by definition, is symbolic. I'm always amazed at how the human brain can interpret any number of squiggles as trees, for instance, as long as there's a line for a trunk underneath. We recognize far more elaborate and individualized symbolism than our alphabets (cursive writing is a form of line drawing), so why not see how expressive that communication can be? If you find drawing intimidating, try my suggestions under "Loosening up for machine embroidery" (p. 120).

What you'll need—To make the transition from drawing lines to sewing them, just think of the needle as a fixed pencil and the fabric as a piece of paper moving underneath. Disengaging the machine's feed dogs by covering, lowering, or removing them enables you to guide the fabric manually in any direction without turning it as you stitch. You can remove the presser foot altogether if you hold the fabric down taut against the bed and right next to the needle with your fingers or if you stretch it in a hoop. If you hold the fabric loosely, the stitches will skip. Thin metal hoops that slide under the needle and are easy to adjust are available at sewing-machine stores.

I prefer to use a darning foot, like the one on my machine (left-hand photo, p. 120), and available for all machines. It moves up and down with the needle, holding the fabric in place just as the stitch is forming, then releasing it to move. With the darning foot I can hold the fabric farther away from the needle, with my hands flat on the fabric for maximum control and freedom of movement. I'm not limited to the space within a hoop, and the thread tension stays more even. These are important factors in achieving easy, flowing lines.

I've graduated from my old Kenmore to an industrial machine, the Chandler long-arm darner (right-hand photo, p. 120), which does exactly what I need and nothing else. It has a moving darning foot and no feed dogs, but it's the 30-in. arm and the 3-ft. x 6-ft. table it's set into that makes stitching bed-size quilts in one piece much easier. However, for years the Kenmore did the job, and I still occasionally use an old straight-stitch Singer with good results. The most important thing for truly free movement is a machine that is set into a table so the bed is flush with the top. Otherwise, it's harder to keep the layers from shifting.

Putting line drawings on fabric—Technically, this hand-guided darning method is called free-machine embroidery. It works best with thick or layered fabrics; thin fabrics will pucker unless they are kept very taut, though machines, and embroiderers, vary. Some people do beautiful machine-embroidery work on lightweight fabrics. My machine prefers cotton thread, and I tend to use all-cotton fabric, but I've never noticed any problems when I use a blend.

When you're ready to start, make sure the presser-foot lever is down so the top-thread tension is engaged. Hold the top thread while stitching in place two or three times to lock the first stitches; then push the fabric at a steady pace under the needle wherever you want to go. If the machine skips stitches, it's probably because the fabric is moving up and down too much with the needle. The tension will vary with changes in speed unless you're an expert, so use the same thread in the spool and bobbin. On most machines you'll have to tighten the top tension a bit to keep the stitches looking good. Practice will help you match how fast the machine goes with how fast you must push the fabric to get roughly uniform stitches, but work toward establishing speed. The faster the needle moves, the easier it is to move the fabric steadily and easily, and the easier it is to get small, even stitches.

I frequently draw the lines that I want to follow directly on the fabric with water-

From *Threads* magazine (December 1988) 20:30-33

With free-motion embroidery techniques, the sewing machine becomes a tool for drawing and quilting simultaneously. Damaris Jackson integrates machine embroidery within traditional quilting structures in "Four-Block Park" (62 in. x 54 in.). In the central blocks of this piece, Jackson's playful stitched white and colored lines make a strong impact on the dark ground. In the border, her stitching takes on a hide-and-seek quality in the vine motifs on the floral print. (Photo by Christine Benkert)

For maximum control and maneuverability, Jackson's Singer is set flush into a table (left). Jackson keeps her hands flat on the fabric and her arms on the table so that her movement is unrestricted. Her industrial darning machine (above) boasts a 30-in. arm and a 3-ft. x 6-ft. table, ideal for large-scale machine quilting. (Photos by Sher Stoneman)

Loosening up for machine embroidery

The idea of drawing is so loaded in many people's minds that it's hard for them to playfully experiment with it. In my workshops I've noticed that some people are naturally more free with the sewing machine as their drawing tool, while others work more easily with a pencil, but there's no question that playing with a pen or pencil can inspire and simplify your machine-embroidered projects. Here are several ways I've approached making line drawings on paper. For adapting these to machine work, try to use a single line as long as possible, but in the end it's up to you if you use two or three lines instead.

1. For outline drawings, trace or draw from a picture or photo, from memory, or from real life.

2. Look at something and try to draw the important parts with one line. What can be left out? What happens if you look at the object, *not* at the paper, and don't lift your pencil until you're done?

3. Adapt a picture. Take a simple drawing (e.g., a cartoon character) or a traditional quilting design, like a sun, and try to work out a way to follow it without lifting your pencil. If you need to skip or add a line, look for a place that isn't too obvious. Often it looks fine to retrace, doubling the line for short distances.

4. Experiment with textures and patterns to see what a line can do: spirals, meanders, zigzags, intersections, etc. Try filling a whole page with a line of one quality.

5. Fill a page with squiggles and see if any one of them looks like something else. Can you make it look even more like that object by changing it just a little? Remember that distortion is a form of expression. Drawings don't have to mimic real life to communicate.

6. Doodle when you're on the phone or when you aren't in the mood to think.

7. Draw from memory. Choose one or more identifying features of your subject and put them in your drawing. For example, thorns turn a nondescript flower into a rose. A four-legged animal with a long, sharp nose is a dog rather than a cat. The texture and shape of the line you use says something about what you're drawing. What does a cat made up of geometric lines say next to one made up of curves?

The key to success is to refrain from making hasty judgments. Finish something even if you don't like it. Eventually, you'll fix it or change it into something else; or you'll get ideas about how to improve on it or what you'd rather do next time. Make a lot of quick drawings. Put them away and look at them later. You'll be surprised at how much more they tell you when you look at them with a fresh perspective. Have fun!

An excellent self-teaching drawing book that has been used with great success by many people who "can't draw" is Betty Edwards's *Drawing on the Right Side of the Brain* (J.P. Tarcher, 1979). —D.J.

soluble pencil or white chalk (colored chalk may not come out), especially if the design is large, and I can't see all of it while I'm at the machine. Chalk comes off with a fabric brush, and a damp rag removes the water-soluble marks. If I'm particularly familiar with a design, I might simplify the general shape to be sure of the placement—for example, two circles for a sheep and a stick for a tree. Sometimes I just wing it. For intricate and hard-to-transfer designs, you can trace the design onto tissue paper, pin the paper in place, stitch along the design, and rip the paper off along the stitching lines. Tweezers will get the last bit out of the seams.

As I'm stitching the design, I often add more details. Seeing the stitched line usually makes me see the design in a new way and makes me want to add new things. The thread is thinner than the chalk line and seems more mobile; I also take more risks when I'm seeing the results up close.

Making quilts—The type of batting that you use in a quilted project is an important consideration. Thin batting needs closer quilting than high-loft batting, and cotton batting needs closer quilting than poly batting. I find that 80% cotton batting is nice for clothing because it is thin and mostly natural, and it washes better than 100% cotton batting. It doesn't slip against the fabric, so I don't need many pins (I never baste). Thin batting is preferable on small pieces because they are more likely to lie flat and be reasonably square when they are finished.

All quilting shrinks the finished size of the piece somewhat, usually more in the middle than at the corners, which makes the edges wrinkle. You can correct this by trimming and adding a separate binding later. On large pieces, shrinkage isn't critical. I usually cut the back of large pieces 1 in. or so bigger than the front, and I bring it around to the front, folding and top-stitching it to make a self-binding before I draw on the design. This is much easier than binding later because it's very hard to mark and sew a straight line on the edge of puffy batting. Then I distribute pins around (about one pin every 12 in.) to keep the back in line with the front.

The main problem with high-loft or slippery batting is that you're likely to get some pinches in the backing. It helps to take the pins out about 3 in. before getting to them. Then, reach under and smooth out the back. If there's a lot of excess fabric built up on the top or bottom, something is wrong, and you need to find the problem and fix it, but a little bit is not unusual. It also helps to complete one area at a time and to do bigger designs before more detailed, confined areas.

If stitching lines traveling across large, open areas don't cross each other, or if the stitching doesn't go all the way to the border, there's less likelihood of pinching. If there's a discrepancy between the size of the back and front, the puffy batting will take up the slack, given room. The pinching problem tends to go away with practice. I figure that the danger of a few small pinches comes with the territory, so I often disguise them by using print fabrics on the back. After all, what other method allows you to make a lovely, original hanging or a baby quilt in less than three hours?

Working with color—It's best to start with one plain colored fabric and one contrasting thread color because that's the easiest way to ensure that you'll be able to read the stitching line as a drawing. Working with more than one color of fabric or thread takes some experimenting. When I've tried to use more than one color, I've found that the same thread may look radically different when it crosses over a second fabric, that threads close in color won't look different unless they're densely stitched, and that contrasting thread colors show up better if there's also a contrast in value (light to dark).

When I want more color, I try to add other color elements beside thread or background fabrics. In "Four-Block Park" (photo, p. 119), I used a black background with white, red, and blue stitching. The white describes the important shapes and figures, while the red and blue fill in and add texture and variety. If I had used white to fill in and color to outline, only the insides of the figures would have shown up. I could probably have done more with color in this piece; there is always more to learn.

Going further—What else can you do with free-machine embroidery? You can draw with the machine on hot pads and pillow covers, screens and fabric yardage. You can put delicate drawings on clothing. Embellishments with soft sculpture or fabric paint can add to the effect. The list is endless.

I get many ideas for projects by asking myself questions: Is it possible to design stitching that holds its own against print fabric? Will appliqué interrupt the flow of the drawings? Can I use close, busy stitching and still have a recognizable picture? What about combining stitched drawings with space-filling stitched patterns? Are the lines interesting at a distance as well as close up? What's the difference between a design that's wearable for everyday clothing and one that's dressy? Don't be afraid to make mistakes. One always learns from them and discovers more questions.

As I've opened up to traditional quilting, still more questions have arisen. What can I learn from the incredible richness of design and content that women before me have created? How does my work relate to this historical context?

Underlying all this is the personal element. People may not yet categorize free-machine embroidery as art or even as quilting, but they do recognize that it can be expressive, and people should express what is important to them. The work of no two individuals will be alike. I'm curious to see what others come up with. ☐

Damaris Jackson of Minneapolis, MN, has had quilts on exhibit in Japan, Austria, Africa, and the U.S. in the past year. She gives lectures and workshops on creative quilting and is program director of Minnesota Quilters, a 1,000-member guild.

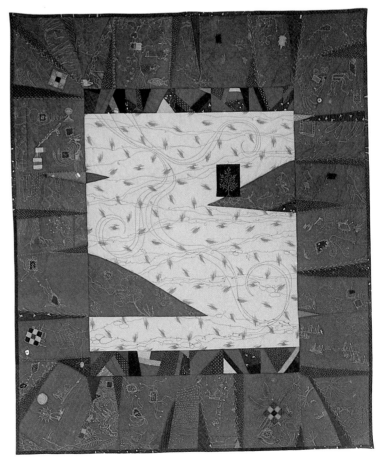

"Lines from the Park" (at right, and detail above), 98 in. x 88 in., was included in Quilt National 1987. Over a crazy-quilt-based background, Jackson freely improvised, without prior sketches or guidelines, all of the machine-quilted line drawings, evoking both her experiences in a neighborhood park and the elaborate hand-embroidery of the 19th-century crazy quilts. (Photo by Christine Benkert)

Work Spaces for Quilting

Inside three stitchers' home studios

by Mary Mashuta

a room of one's own . . . a place to work . . . a place you don't have to clean up before the project is done. . . . This is a common desire among "needle people." I've been pleased to see that many quilters are reaching the point in their careers where they are ready to carve out permanent work spaces in their own homes.

There are some common misconceptions that might be preventing you from claiming a special space for quilting in your home. The first is that unless you can have a whole room exclusively to yourself, you can't have your own home studio. On the other hand, if you are fortunate enough to

possess a room, you may assume that it should and will solve all your work-space problems. Many times there just isn't enough space in our modern homes and apartments for all the activities that we'd like to carry on. Often rooms become multipurpose; compromise is frequently a necessity.

Regardless of the space you have, it's important to have a clear idea of what you'll be doing there. As a rule, you'll need places to design and draft, cut out, sew, press, and quilt. As you create projects, you'll need a way to view them as works in progress so you can think about them visually.

You'll also need to think about storing your equipment and supplies. Grouping

things that are used together makes sense. Locate them as close as possible to where they'll be used. If you run out of space, decide which items can be stored elsewhere in your house. Finished quilts, for example, are very bulky. It's more important to give the space available in your studio to your fabric collection. Solutions can be found for every budget. You can order custom-

Bernice McCoy Stone's basket collection stores supplies, like batting and current projects. Baskets hang with large S-hooks from a ceiling-mounted pole. The design pinup area on the wall at right holds inspirational images or fabric choices for quilts in progress.

made worktables or start off with doors from the lumberyard. Establishing priorities will help make compromise easier.

For purposes of comparison, I've selected studios that vary considerably in appearance, size, and investment. Each of the artists has created a solution that fits into her lifestyle, way of working, space available, and budget. Perhaps one of their solutions will encourage you to create, adapt, or perfect a space you've been considering.

Bernice McCoy Stone

Bernice spends up to 40 hours a week making traditional appliqué and pieced quilts. She is an avid quilt collector who enjoys sharing her quilts with local guilds.

Bernice has claimed as her studio a small upstairs room (shown in the photo at left) that had belonged to her son, but her quilting spreads beyond the confines of this room. The guest room provides storage for some of her quilts in the dresser and closet. More quilts are stored in the Bicentennial Room. In this upstairs sitting room, furnished in antiques, she can set up her quilt frame where it won't interfere with other household activities. When Bernice really gets going, she likes to switch to a schedule of working 4 hours, sleeping 4 hours, working 4 hours, etc. A home studio is perfect for her because her spaces are available 24 hours a day.

Bernice had her studio room enlarged years ago by incorporating space taken up by a hallway and two closets (see floor plan at right). It has four built-in bookcases and a small storage closet. She also added an antique chest with many small drawers. Bernice has three tables that serve as work surfaces, where she can design, draft, cut out, stitch, and press her patchwork and appliqué blocks. Her Bernina sewing machine is on a 32½-in.-high custom-made table; it's more comfortable for her than a standard sewing-machine table, which varies from 29 in. to 31 in. The machine is set into the table, and a portion of the front edge drops so that the bobbin can be inserted. There are two cubbyholes in the front apron for sewing-machine attachment trays. She was able to stretch the work surface by pairing it in an L with a parson's table she already had.

Bernice still does a lot of machine piecing on her old Singer Featherweight portable. Since it's set up on the parson's table, it's easy for her to pivot around to it on her secretarial chair. By moving the Singer to the end of the parson's table and providing another secretarial chair, she can comfortably invite another quilter to join her.

So she can easily locate sewing notions and tools while near the machines, Bernice has attached two 24-in. x 18-in. Heller grids (from Heller Designs, 41 Madison Ave., New York, NY 10010; 1-800-223-0750) to the corner walls to the right of the machines. Various hooks, baskets, and shelves can be attached so a large variety of small

items can be stored. At a local import store, Bernice found French bread baskets made of metal and added them to one of the grids. They're perfect for storing rulers and individual patchwork pieces. She collects drafting tools in other baskets and stores sets of large plastic and metal quilters' rulers in an antique churn and an antique crock on the floor nearby.

Bernice's sister Emily made her a small pressing board to place on the tabletop to the right of her machine. With this setup, she can stitch pieces together and immediately press them without getting up and walking over to an ironing board.

As the projects grow larger, or when additional quilters are in the room, Bernice takes the ironing board out of the closet. To prevent her from tripping over iron cords, her husband rigged up a ceiling-mounted drapery rod. Coiled, expandable extension cords are caught into drapery-hook glides so they can travel the length of the rod. When the iron is plugged in, she can move it from place to place without worrying about where the cord is.

Since there weren't enough electrical outlets, Bernice had an electrician add five double outlets across the back of the sewing-center worktables. Now she doesn't have to crawl under the table to reach them.

The third table in the room was originally made to be used as a 40-in.-high stand-up worktable. After using the table for a while, she found that it was hard to get good leverage when she was using her rotary cutter, so she had the legs cut down to 35 in. Now she can work at the table while sitting in her secretarial chair. Under the table a modular wire-drawer unit holds fabric and works in progress.

On the wall behind the table, a piece of 4-ft. x 8-ft. Celotex insulation board, available at lumberyards, is Molly-bolted horizontally to the wall, creating a design pin-up area. A felt covering allows small pieces of fabric to adhere during the designing process. If Bernice wants to put up all the blocks of a large quilt, she expands this board with a piece of Pellon fleece that she can pin to. When she's not using the board for designing, she decorates it with individual blocks or design inspirations.

Bernice's fabric collection is folded and stored in the bookcases, along with her quilt library. Scraps of fabric are organized by color in small plastic baskets.

To light her work area, Bernice has mounted incandescent track lighting on the ceiling in a T configuration. The track comes in 4-ft. modules that can be connected to each other or cut smaller. The five fixtures can be moved around and tilted in position. Fluorescent fixtures would generate less heat and use less electricity, but they cost more to install.

A small allover-print wallpaper in a light value and a white vinyl-tile floor for easy upkeep help brighten the room. It's hard to find the perfect studio floor covering. The

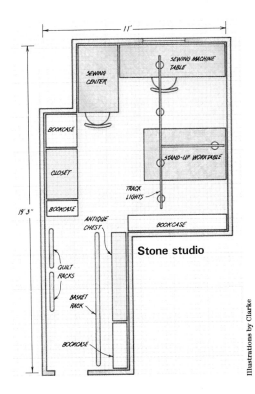

Stone studio

casters on the secretarial chairs have marked the floor. Hard-surface secretarial pads are available, but they limit movement.

Bernice has created a warm, charming home studio where she can joyfully spend her retirement years surrounded by her quilting projects. Best of all, it is always available, day or night.

Marinda Brown Stewart

Marinda creates both limited-edition and one-of-a-kind wearables, wholesales a line of garment patterns, and works as a freelance designer. She coordinates fashion shows and teaches workshops. Even though she doesn't make quilts, many of her concerns are shared by quilters who are interested in wearables.

Marinda needs cut-out, sewing, and pressing centers for garment construction. She wants a place to store fabric, patterns, and assorted sewing, embroidery, and knitting supplies. She needs a work center to assemble, package, and prepare for mailing the kits she retails and wholesales. She needs somewhere to work on business correspondence and do the art work and paste-ups for her pattern business. Her library has to be readily available.

Marinda has had her own studio space for nine years. The present setup, the smaller bedroom in a two-bedroom apartment, is the fourth rendition. It is also the smallest. Since she opted for the luxury of a large master bedroom, she has had to use part of the space in that room for the overflow from her 10-ft. x 11-ft. studio. In the master bedroom she keeps her desk, drafting table, some of her books, and a portable garment rack.

By having the sliding closet doors removed and the closet area converted into a sewing alcove, Marinda was able to increase the usable space in the small studio

Marinda Brown Stewart had closet doors removed in order to create a sewing area in her 10-ft. x 11-ft. second bedroom (top). She stores fabric and supplies under her plywood worktable, using inexpensive modular units that raise the table to a comfortable 32 in. (above).

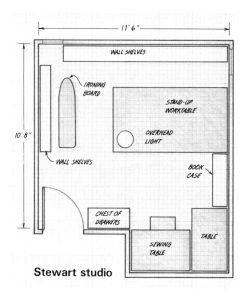

Stewart studio

(see floor plan at left, below). A Bernina sewing machine and a serger are always ready on the L-shaped work space (top photo). Bricks elevate the standard sewing-machine table to 32 in., which helps alleviate backaches aggravated by long hours of sewing. The pegboard above the serger displays sewing implements and makes them easy to find. An inexpensive fluorescent shop light supplies task lighting. Overhead, two shelves provide storage for bulky items, such as batting, pillow forms, and yarns.

Marinda uses the stand-up worktable, shown in the lower photo, for cutting out garments and assembling and packaging her patterns. The top is a 4-ft. x 8-ft. piece of plywood. Trimmed to 45 in. to fit in the small room, it accommodates the width of most fabrics. At one end of the tabletop, Marinda displays fabric that she is currently excited about.

The table incorporates storage space underneath. Fabric is boxed by color or stored in four inexpensive, two-drawer, 16-in. x 32-in. chipboard modular units from an unfinished-furniture store. There is still space under the table to place miscellany, like gift wrap and a knitting machine, and to store embroidery thread and supplies in a small chest of drawers.

Near the worktable is the ironing board, always available for pressing because it's left in an upright position. A clip-on spotlight, attached to one of the board-and-bracket shelves above, adds task lighting.

Individual "clutter tolerances" vary. Marinda enjoys filling her room and surrounding herself with stuff that she feels strongly about. Mementos that family members have crafted share space with inspirational materials for pieces yet to be designed.

A serious drawback of the room is that its size doesn't permit Marinda to view items from a distance as she creates them. Consequently, projects may spread beyond the studio. High on the priority list for new acquisitions is a dress form, which would allow Marinda to view her garments three-dimensionally as she creates them.

All things considered, Marinda feels she has come up with the most efficient arrangement of her belongings so far. She concludes that "you work with what you have, not necessarily with what you want." She has arranged her furnishings and equipment so everything is at her fingertips. Her system has become streamlined and more functional with time.

Roberta Horton

Our last quilter is a person I'm particularly well acquainted with, since she's my sister and housemate. She's internationally known as a lecturer, a teacher, an author, and a quiltmaker. A busy teaching schedule keeps her away from home for a good part of the year. An organized work space is a necessity for the time she spends at home.

When we purchased our house 12 years ago, studio space was one of the criteria in our selection. The large dining room became "The Studio," but the room was never ideal for designing quilts, because it was impossible to have a permanent pinup wall area. We definitely outgrew the space when a computer was added. In 1984, we converted a 10-ft. x 16-ft. upstairs junk room to an additional studio. The dining room was officially designated "Studio A"; the second space, "Studio B." Studio A was for correspondence and writing, preparing slide lectures and workshops, and quilting on the large quilting frame. Studio B was for designing and sewing quilt tops.

Things worked fairly well until I quit my teaching job and became a full-time quilter. During the summer of 1986 we decided that a third studio was the only solution, so we began reevaluating the space in our house. Options we had always supposed we had evaporated under close scrutiny. We finally decided to have a 12-ft. x 17-ft. addition built on the back of the house. Studio C would be Roberta's dream work space.

Roberta decided to locate her quilt designing and construction work center and her writing and slide-sorting center in the proposed Studio C. She needed close-at-hand storage for an extensive fabric collection and basic tools. She wanted oak tables and cupboards rather than the metal office tables and vinyl-coated particle-board bookcases we used in Studio B. She also wanted a large bulletin board to display inspirational materials.

As Roberta's plans for her dream studio began to jell, compromise entered the picture. To enlarge an adjacent bathroom, we had to relocate the washer and dryer. The only solution was to put them in the storage closet of the new studio. However, it was easy to create a bulletin board on the plain surface of the doors that were concealing the appliances.

Two file-drawer units and a bookshelf were added to the table we used as the communications/writing center, shown in the top photo, facing page. Adjoining this work area are the two tables that make up the design/construction center. Here, Roberta can sketch, cut out fabric with her Olfa cutter and mat, machine-sew, and press small pieces of patchwork on her portable ironing board. A 4-in.-high stand raises her Singer Featherweight to help ease neck and shoulder strain she experienced from bending over a too-low machine.

On the wall nearby, a 24-in. x 36-in. Heller grid stores thread, sewing notions, and drafting supplies. On the wall directly across the room are two 4-ft. x 8-ft. felt-covered Celotex boards, as in Bernice's studio, creating a design wall, shown in the drawing and accompanying photo on the facing page.

The black-and-white asphalt tiles had held up well in Studio B, so Roberta decided to use them here too. They provide a rigid surface for the secretarial chair's casters. The 12-in.-sq. tiles also create a large grid

for Roberta to use in estimating quilt size and trueing up completed projects. The Benjamin Moore Spanish White wall paint in Studio B had proved to be a pleasing neutral background, so we decided to repeat it.

Roberta and I devoted a lot of thought to light-safe fabric storage. Like most quilters, Roberta has a large, valuable fabric collection, assembled over many years. After displaying her collection in open bookcases for several years, fabric edges began to fade. This was probably caused by exposure to fluorescent light rather than by light coming through the window in Studio B, because the window had been coated with solar film and covered with a pleated Z shade, both of which reduce ultraviolet light.

Vitalite full-spectrum fluorescent bulbs (from Duro-lite Lamps, 1050 Wall St. W., Lyndhurst, NJ 07071; 1-800-526-7193) provide true-color, inexpensive lighting, making Studio C an inviting place for evening work. As an added precaution, Roberta had Solar Control Window Film (from Martin Processing, Consumer Products, Box 5068, Martinsville, VA 24115; 703-629-1711) applied to the interior glass surface of the cupboard doors and to the window. We've just ordered ultraviolet filtering fluorescent-bulb sleeves that will offer further protection (from Solar Screen, 53-11 105th St., Corona, NY 11368; 718-592-8222).

Another problem with storing fabric over a long period of time is that it can discolor and weaken from constant contact with an acidic wood surface. A textile conservator suggested lining the cabinets with aluminum foil, an inert substance. Paint or Varathane will also seal the wood. If you're using cardboard boxes or unsealed-chipboard modular units, consider a foil lining. You can also use acid-free tissue paper, which is available through many quilt stores. It is heavier than regular tissue paper and won't tear as easily.

Now we each have our own separate studio. Two quilters can share a house, but each needs her own work space. Over time, Studio B will look more and more like me as pictures and mementos are revamped. The first major change has been a new stand-up work table. The room is small, so I selected the Sew & Craft Versatility Table (from Seth Products, 2985 Dutton Ave., #10, Santa Rosa, CA 95407, 1-800-443-7433; outside CA, 1-800-331-6529). The top consists of segments so it can be set up in three sizes. The height adjusts from 22 in. to 39 in. It weighs only 14 lb., can be stored in an area 10 in. x 24 in. x 44 in., and has wheels, making it easy to move.

Given some thought, and with the shared experience of fellow artists, outfitting and organizing a work space can be almost as enjoyable as using it. ☐

Mary Mashuta of Berkeley, Ca, in addition to creating story quilts and wearable art, gives lectures and workshops on them and on work-space solutions.

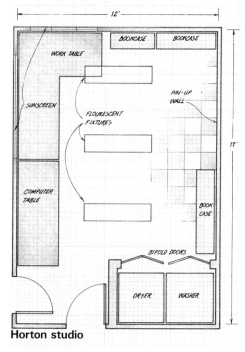

Horton studio

Quilt author Roberta Horton provided ample space for word-processing equipment in her recently completed studio (top). The windows have been treated and screened to reduce fabric-fading ultraviolet-light levels. Above, she auditions a border fabric for a quilt project on her design wall—two sheets of Celotex covered with felt. Fabric is safely stored behind glass, also treated to screen ultraviolet light.

A designer's strategies

How would a professional organizer approach your quilting room? We asked Paula Lasken, a designer for California Closets, how she thinks about other people's spaces. Here's what she told us.

"Most people have no idea how much stuff they own. The first step in any serious reorganization is a detailed inventory. The next step, which everybody leaves out, is to actually measure what you need to store: How wide, deep, and high is it? Then measure your storage space. If it won't fit, something has to go. We've found that the optimum size for shelves is 14 in. deep by 32 in. wide between supports. Any deeper, and you can't get to the stuff in back; any wider, and the shelves will sag. Stacks of folded cloth, whether fabric, linens, or clothes, seem to average 14 in. on a side.

When you're planning working space, start by mapping out traffic flow. How will you need to move to get from work station to station, to windows and doors? At each station, what do you need to get to without reaching or changing position? Block out your movements at each station—you have to plan space for yourself!

Finally, if room is tight, take heart. Small spaces are easier to organize, and they're usually more efficient than big spaces."

Index

If you enjoyed this book, you're going to love our magazine.

A year's subscription to *THREADS* brings you the kind of hands-on information you found in this book, and much more. In issue after issue - six times a year - you'll find articles on sewing, needlecrafts and textile arts. Artists and professionals will share their best techniques and trade secrets with you. With detailed illustrations and full-color photographs that bring each project to life, *THREADS* will inspire you to create your best work ever!

To subscribe, just fill out one of the attached subscription cards or call us at 1-203-426-8171. And as always, your satisfaction is guaranteed, or we'll give you your money back.

The Taunton Press
63 S. Main Street, Box 5506, Newtown, CT 06470-5506

Eleanor Burns
Holiday Series
1-800-U2-Kwilt

19.95 + 4⁰⁰